THE SCIENCE OF LOVE
AND OTHER WRITINGS

THE SCIENCE OF LOVE
AND OTHER WRITINGS

....

CHARLES CROS

TRANSLATED BY DOUG SKINNER

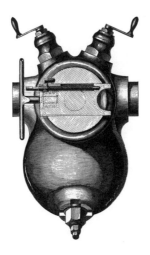

WAKEFIELD PRESS, CAMBRIDGE, MASSACHUSETTS

Wakefield Press, P.O. Box 425645, Cambridge, MA 02142

This book was set in Garamond Premier Pro and Helvetica Neue Pro by Wakefield Press. Printed and bound by Sheridan Saline, Inc., in the United States of America.

ISBN: 978-1-939663-95-5

Available through D.A.P./Distributed Art Publishers
75 Broad Street, Suite 630
New York, New York 10004
Tel: (212) 627-1999
Fax: (212) 627-9484

10   9   8   7   6   5   4   3   2   1

CONTENTS

TRANSLATOR'S INTRODUCTION

Charles Cros (1842–1888) was an unusually complex figure, even by the standards of fin-de-siècle Paris. He pursued a double career as scientist and writer, brilliant in both yet unable to make money from either. One of his friends, Émile Goudeau, said of him "Rarely was any man more gifted," and called him "a winged being, gathering a bit of dew and honey from the flowers, with no desire to condense any useful sap from them."[1]

Hortensius-Émile-Charles Cros (or Émile-Hortensius-Charles Cros; reports vary) belonged to a family of writers and artists. His grandfather, Antoine Cros, translated Theocritus, and his father, Simon-Charles-Henri Cros, wrote a weighty *Theory of Intellectual and Moral Man*. Charles was the youngest of four siblings: the eldest, Antoine, was by turns physician, poet, and philosopher; a sister, Henriette, was the second (of whom little is known); and the third, Henry, devoted himself to painting and ceramics.

The family was poor, and Simon himself schooled his children. As a child, Charles learned several languages (reportedly Greek, Latin, Sanskrit, Hebrew, German, and Italian, although it's difficult to tell how well), and studied mathematics and music. At eighteen, he was hired as a teaching assistant at a school for the deaf in Paris, only to be fired for implication in a duel. After studying and then abandoning medicine, he joined his brothers in exploring the salons and cafés of Paris.

There he met Nina de Callias. She was pale and plump, with large expressive eyes and masses of black hair. "Ah! What a strange little fairy was that Nina, so mad, so laughing, so amusing," Edmond Lepelletier later wrote.[2] She hosted a salon that attracted such celebrities as Pierre-Auguste Renoir, Paul Cézanne, Stéphane Mallarmé, Paul Verlaine, Richard Wagner, and Édouard Manet (who painted a memorable portrait of her). The salon also gained a reputation as an open house where any poor artist could help himself to the bar and buffet. "No need for a dress suit to be received at my house, a sonnet is enough," she said.[3]

She was born Anne-Marie Gaillard, into a rich family in Lyon, in 1843. Her principal interest was music; a few of her compositions were published, and she had a reputation as an excellent pianist. In 1864, she married Count Hector de Callias, a journalist and dandy given to pearl-gray and peach-blossom suits. The marriage lasted only three years, marked by frequent quarrels, often provoked by his hatred of music (he once threw the key to her piano out the window). They separated, but never divorced, and she took her mother's maiden name, becoming Nina de Villard. Hector continued his career as a theater and art critic, punctuated by frequent arrests for public intoxication.

In Nina's salon, Cros met poets of the Parnassian movement, such as Mallarmé and Verlaine. Rejecting Romanticism, they followed Théophile Gautier's edict of "art for art's sake," with its emphasis on craftsmanship, and admired Théodore de Banville's experiments with rhyme and meter. The Parnassians' work was collected in three anthologies published by Alphonse Lemerre in 1866, 1871, and 1876. Both Charles and Nina started writing poetry around this time, and each contributed two poems to the second anthology.

They also began a long, intermittent, and stormy love affair, which was to last until 1877 and would inspire much of Cros's poetry.

Their artistic and personal interests were interrupted by the Franco-Prussian War. The Cros's house was bombed by the Germans, and the family sought refuge with Madame Mauté de Fleurville, Verlaine's mother-in-law. The Commune followed in 1871; Cros served the rebellion as an aide major. Nina and her mother escaped to Geneva during those years.

When some semblance of normal life resumed, Cros and his brothers joined the Vilains Bonshommes, a loose literary club into which Verlaine introduced Rimbaud. After Rimbaud was expelled for shouting "merde" during other poets' readings, dissenting members formed the Cercle Zutique. Under the direction of Ernest Cabaner, the cadaverous pianist of the Hôtel des Étrangers, they amused themselves with smutty parodies of more successful poets. Among Charles's contributions was a pornographic mono-syllabic sonnet about Tristan and Isolde, which defies translation. Rimbaud stayed with Charles during this time, showing his usual tact by destroying his laboratory and tearing up his writings.

In 1872, the poets Émile Blémont and Jean Aicard started a new magazine, *La Renaissance littéraire et artistique*, with the back-ing of Victor Hugo. As the title indicates, it hoped to revive French art and literature after the upheavals of the war and the Commune. One of its hallmarks was its approach to art criticism, based on Baudelaire's dictum that "the best criticism is that which is amus-ing and poetic. . . . The best description of a painting could be a sonnet or an elegy."[4] Again, both Charles and Nina contributed.

Cros's literary career was well underway. In 1873 he published a collection of his poetry, *Le Coffret de santal* (The sandalwood casket), and a long poem about the Seine, *Le Fleuve* (The river), illustrated by Manet. He even launched his own journal, *La Revue du monde nouveau*, funded by Nina. It lasted for three issues in 1874, printing many of the regulars in Nina's salon.

Throughout all of this, he pursued his varied scientific projects. He had already patented a telegraph and (with his brother Antoine) a stenographic piano, and had written papers on the effect of meteors on tree bark and on communication with other planets, as well as a detailed study entitled *Principles of Cerebral Mechanics*. He attempted color photography, only to have another inventor, Louis Arthur Ducos de Hauron, patent the process before him. In 1877, he submitted a plan for a phonograph, which he called the paléophone—since it preserved sounds from the past—to the Académie des Sciences. This time Thomas Edison beat him to the patent while Cros was still raising money for a prototype. He continued to work on improving color photography, but never achieved anything commercial enough to satisfy his backers. Writing often took second place; as he said, "I persevere with color photography at the moment, but literature lies idle as a result."[5]

His affair with Nina de Villard also ended that year. Shortly afterward, he married another woman, Mary Hjardemaal. He also met two men who were to play important parts in his life, Émile Goudeau and Coquelin Cadet.

Goudeau was a fiery poet, dark, bearded, and markedly strabismic. He started a literary society that he called the Hydropaths, both because they shunned water and because his own name sounded like *goût d'eau* (taste of water). Cros read his own poems to great enthusiasm and wrote a lively drinking song for the meetings. One of his poems, a nonsense verse for children called "The Salt Herring," attracted the attention of the actor Ernest Coquelin. Known as Coquelin Cadet (the younger, to distinguish him from his older brother, also an actor), he was looking for material to use in cabarets and at private parties. Cros agreed to supply him with comic monologues, self-contained character sketches that could be performed anywhere in street clothes. Cros's monologues were something new, a departure from the usual actor's repertory of mock lectures or soliloquies excerpted from plays, and they inspired many imitations. Coquelin, unfortunately, paid him very little for them.

The Hydropathes eventually needed a larger space, so when Rodolphe Salis opened the Chat Noir in 1881, Goudeau and his followers made it their headquarters. Like any self-respecting cabaret, the Chat Noir also published a weekly paper, edited at first by Goudeau, and later by the Hydropathe Alphonse Allais. Allais, like Cros, had a scientific education, having moved to Paris to study pharmacology, only to abandon it for a remarkable career as a comic writer. Encouraged by both Goudeau and Allais, Cros became a frequent contributor.

In his last few years, Cros steadily sank into poverty, illness, and alcoholism. He wrote poetry and fiction for a variety of Parisian journals, patented a chromometer and an improved telegraph, and wrote papers on celestial photography and the mapping of Mars. Still, as he remarked to Goudeau, "Neither fame nor money, it's hard!"[6] He died in 1888 at the age of forty-five, leaving Mary with two children. The younger, René, died young (1880–1898); the elder, Guy-Charles, had a long career as a poet. Guy-Charles also edited a posthumous collection of his father's work, *Le Collier de griffes* (The claw necklace) in 1908, which preserved many fugitive and unpublished pieces.

Nina de Villard had died four years before, in a mental hospital in Vanves. Cros and Hector de Callias were among the few who attended her funeral. Days later, de Callias was seen staggering through the streets, yelling at streetlights, still wearing the same clothes.

Cros's writing took many forms. His poetry is nervous and delicate, usually cast in the strict forms favored by the Parnassians: sonnets, quatrains, and dizains. His prose was written for various reasons and audiences, and includes science fiction, comic pieces, children's stories, prose poems, memoir, and scientific papers.

This collection begins with two of Cros's longer stories, both anticipating science fiction. The first might have been inspired by his quarrels with Nina de Villard, who detested his scientific research to the point of throwing his work into the fire; the clueless narrator might be a self-caricature. In "An Interplanetary Drama," Cros draws on his interests in extraterrestrial communication and in the recording of sensory impressions. "The Newspaper of the Future" projects his colleagues Salis, Allais, and de Banville into the future, incidentally predicting our current fascination with artificial intelligence. "Smoky Diamond" is Cros at his most autobiographical, an aching memoir of Nina de Villard, published after her death. "People of Letters" is either a children's story or a parody of one (the bedroom antics during the ball suggest the latter), which even cites his famous monologue "The Salt Herring."

The prose poem was still a relatively new form in Cros's time. Several of his are descriptions of artworks, as championed by *La*

Renaissance littéraire et artistique: a fantasy on a cabinet owned by Madame Mauté de Fleurville and a series on his brother's aquatints. Others are brief meditations, by turns erotic ("Distractor" and "Madrigal") and melancholy ("The Cold Hour" and "Lassitude").

The scientific writings include the remarkable "Study on Methods of Communication with Other Planets," originally presented to the Académie des Sciences in 1869. His plan was ridiculed at the time, and even today is cited as evidence that Cros was a crackpot. In fact, he was not convinced of the existence of Martians and Venusians, as some critics have charged, but simply thought it possible. His proposal for light signals was impractical, but, as he said, the only feasible solution at the time, and he expected the future would bring better methods. Which it did: by the end of the century, scientists were discussing using radio waves for the purpose, and both Tesla and Marconi reported possible transmissions from Mars. By the middle of the next century, astronomers were actively searching for extraterrestrial signals. One of the first was Frank Drake's "Project Ozma" at Cornell University in 1960, and one of the most sustained was John D. Kraus's SETI program at Ohio State University, which ran from 1973 to 1995. The idea of sending signals into space was attempted with the Arecibo message, designed by Drake and Carl Sagan in 1974, which followed Cros's plan of encoding simple diagrams in binary form.

The last piece in this collection is a patent application for a notating keyboard, invented by Cros with his brother Antoine. It's the earliest of his inventions, and was apparently never built, let alone marketed. It can be read as the first product of his fascination with preserving sensory impressions, later developed in the paléophone, his research into color photography, and the *Principles of Cerebral Mechanics*.

Cros was, as Goudeau said, unusually gifted, and wrote some memorable work. He had the inconvenient gift of being ahead of his time, and the bad luck to die young. I hope this collection allows more readers to discover this unique and brilliant "winged being" of French literature.[7]

NOTES

1. Émile Goudeau, *Dix ans de bohème* (Paris: La Librairie illustrée, 1888), 123, 128.

2. Edmond Lepelletier, *Paul Verlaine: Sa vie, son œuvre* (Paris: Mercure de France, 1907), 171.

3. Marie de Grandfort, "Nina de Villard, comtesse Hector de Callias," *La Grande Revue de Paris et de Saint-Pétersbourg*, 15 October 1888.

4. Baudelaire Dufaÿs (Charles Baudelaire), *Salon de 1846* (Paris: Michel Levy Frères, 1846), 2.

5. Letter from 1880, quoted in "Repères biographiques," *Œuvres complètes de Charles Cros* (Paris: Club des Libraires de France, Pauvert, 1964).

6. Goudeau, *Dix ans de bohème*, 129.

7. For readers interested in more Cros, I have also translated *Principles of Cerebral Mechanics* for Wakefield Press and *Collected Monologues* and *Upside-Down Stories* (the latter written with Émile Goudeau) for Black Scat Books.

THE SCIENCE OF LOVE
AND OTHER WRITINGS

THE SCIENCE OF LOVE

Since my youth, I've possessed a fine fortune and a taste for science. Not that empty science that pretentiously believes it can create the world from scratch, and which flits through the blue atmosphere of the imagination. I've always thought, in agreement with the rigorous cohort of modern scientists, that man is only a stenographer of brutal facts, a secretary of tangible nature; that truth, created not by a few futile universalities, but in an enormous and confused mass, can only be partially accessible to scratchers, gnawers, pryers, messengers, and accumulators of real, verifiable, undeniable facts; in a word, that you must be an ant, mite, rotifer, or vibrio, that you must be nothing in order to bring your own atom to the infinity of atoms that comprise the majestic pyramid of scientific truths. Observe, observe; above all, never think, dream, or imagine: these are the splendors of our current method.

It was with these sound doctrines that I entered life; and, ever since my first steps, a marvelous project, a true scientific opportunity, came into my mind.

When I learned physics, I said to myself:

We've studied weight, heat, electricity, magnetism, and light. The mechanical equivalents of these forces are, or will be, determined incontestably by rigorous means. But all those who work on expressing these elements of future knowledge play only a minor role in the world.

There are other forces that keen and patient observation must submit to the scientist's mind. I won't make broad classifications, because I consider them harmful to study, and because I don't understand them. In short, I was led (how and why, I don't know) to undertake the *scientific* study of love.

I don't have an absolutely disagreeable physique, I'm neither too tall nor too short, and no one has ever claimed my hair was either brown or blond. Only my eyes are a little small, and not bright enough, which gives me a dazed look that's useful in scientific societies, but harmful in society.

About this society, moreover, despite many methodical efforts, I have no clear understanding, and it was a true masterpiece of composure for me to have been able, without drawing attention, to pursue my austere goal.

I said to myself: I want to study love, not like the Don Juans who amuse themselves without writing about it, not like the writers who mistily sentimentalize, but like serious scientists. To record the effect of heat on zinc, you take a bar of zinc and heat it in water at a temperature rigorously determined by the best thermometer possible; you measure precisely the length of the bar, its resistance, its sonority, its heat capacity, and you do the same at another temperature, no less rigorously determined.

It was by equally exact procedures that I proposed to myself (a remarkable project at such a tender age—barely twenty-five) to *study* love. A difficult enterprise.

In general, some irritating and even culpable repugnance leads amorous people to avoid obstinately all scientific examination; and particularly at those moments when examination would be most fruitful. This granted, my plan was very quickly halted.

To study love, I tell myself, I must take the best vantage point. Even the most intimate confidant is dismissed during the characteristic minutes. It is only the furniture, sometimes a dog or cat, that witnesses those mysteries that inexplicable fate has until now withdrawn from analysis. I have then only one resource, namely to play personally the role of lover.

Having scarcely any charms, since the few that nature gave me had declined in the shadows of libraries and odors of laboratories, I resorted to my profound knowledge to make myself worthy of feminine dreams.

Oh, the marvelous cosmetics, insoluble youthful rouge, bluish black of sleepless eyes, oils to make my skin diaphanous, and galvanizations to shape my legs, that I invented at the time! But I was not naive enough to count solely on the appearance of my face, or on the allure of my physique. I needed to master those charming nothings that seduce young women, those ridiculous futilities that the finer sex imposes upon us.

I went to see Chopin and asked him, "You've played the piano a great deal in society. What music do women like best?"

He replied without hesitation, "Rosellen's 'Reverie.'"

"Forty thousand francs, if you're willing to teach me to play that reverie perfectly."

Chopin, ridiculously impractical, recused himself and recommended M. K***, one of his students, as better than he (which was true, anyway). M. K*** accepted the forty thousand francs and, true to his word, taught me to play nothing but Rosellen's "Reverie."

I was armed on that front.

I went to see Musset and asked him: "What poetry do women like best?"

Musset placed his forefinger on his eyebrow and said, "Acrostics."

"Here's fifty thousand francs, teach me acrostics."

Musset, incorrigible bohemian, didn't understand that I was his providence, and sent me to M. W*** (I prefer not to reveal his name), a student whom I thought better than his teacher.

W*** took the fifty thousand francs and wrote for me an exquisite collection of acrostics, on all the names of feminine martyrology. Each name had three versions: blonde, brunette, and light brown. I also received a written promise of delivery for unexpected cases. Thus armed, I resolutely entered society.

After numerous failures (so true it is that one learns only by experiment), failures pointless to describe, I finally found my affair. It was in a family living in the Marais, in one of those old buildings fit for a Speaker of Parliament.

The entire ground floor served as a stationery store, and on the great stone staircase with its patiently forged banister you mounted interminable steps to the upper floor, where M. D*** and his family lived. The honest neglected look of the house pleased me at once the first time I went there.

M. D*** had given the stationery store below to his older daughter's husband. Previously, a pen at his ear and his eye on the merchandise, he'd acquired a fortune substantial enough to ensure a reasonable dowry for his younger daughter, while being careful not to irritate the "hopes" of his sons-in-law.

They received every Saturday. Modest little receptions, tea, little cakes, etc. It was to marry their daughter that they indulged in these simple joys, and, in addition, took the aforesaid daughter around to all the houses of their peers. I'd traveled through an enormous number of those interiors, conscientiously hopping to the noises of the polkas and quadrilles that complacent mamas sweated from their flabby fingers. As I was seen everywhere, I succeeded in getting invited to the D*** family. I'd decided, after comparative examinations, that Mlle D***'s complexion was, more than any other young lady proposed, suitable for my plans.

My position was excellent. I was received in view of a possible marriage; therefore they paid attention to me; I was emphasized, adroitly, in a way not to discourage the possibly capricious young lady.

But I had my fixed plan. It being of ancient notoriety that marriage has nothing to do with love, I had to maneuver to avoid this disastrous conclusion, which I'd already been offered several times, and which I'd always escaped, not without compromising myself to some extent.

I began by giving the mother some advice on the subject of her excessive corpulence, all within the limits of the most exquisite politeness and even the most innocent goodwill, of course.

This advice caused her voice to assume a bittersweet tone, and provoked a political profession of faith to which I offered some reservations. I left it there, however, not wanting to rush things, and began to chat, with a somewhat sad and preoccupied air, with the young lady. I stopped in the middle of sentences that even the Devil couldn't have finished, any more than I:

"There are cases where the soul must rise above complexities..."

Or:

"The heart is a slave whose chains ... The heart is a slave who cannot obey ..., etc."

Then, after a sigh, I seated myself at the piano, and Rosellen's irresistible "Reverie" earned me delicious looks of submission over the shoulder of the young lady pouring the tea.

Her name was Virginie, and her hair was light brown. My collection of acrostics included this particular case, in the form you can read here:

> Vague fevered dreams, too numerous to name,
> Inexorably setting us aflame,
> Repel us from the chattering salon.
> Grant me one glance (for your celestial blue
> Intoxicates me), and I live anew,
> Naive and fond of trees. Let us begone!
> It's time you left your life and parents here,
> Embracing me in place of them, my dear.

These verses, corrected by my friend the poet W*** according to the situation, lent themselves marvelously to my plans for abduction. As soon as I'd adroitly slipped them into Virginie's moist hand, the poor girl was under my power.

One evening, taking my cup of tea, I pressed her little fingers beneath the saucer. From emotion, or perhaps intention on my part, the cup fell, broke on the corner of the piano, and the tea, boiling, sugared, with its cloud of milk, soaked my superb pearl-gray trousers.

"How clumsy I am!" I said, paling under the burn, which was insignificant anyway. "I've ruined your dress, mademoiselle."

"That's all you ever do, Virginie," said the mother.

"Madame, I assure you it was my fault, when I set the cup on the edge of the piano . . ."

"Besides, the maid can serve the tea and cordials."

The young lady disappeared. Oh, if I could have witnessed the night she must have spent!

In short, I calibrated my actions and gestures so well that the parents' antagonism grew at the same rate as the daughter's love. Subsequently, I exchanged a few whispered words with the young woman: she was unhappy, her parents detested me . . . they needed to be handled carefully, etc.

I seem to be writing a novel, but it would be a mistake to think me so frivolous. What I've said here, as briefly as possible, was necessary. Now science, in the proper sense of the word, can begin.

We exchanged our portraits. Mine was a photograph on enamel, framed in gold, with a minuscule chain, to be worn under the clothes.

The portrait contained, concealed between an ivory plaque and the enamel, two maximum and minimum thermometers, two masterpieces of precision at such a small scale.

Thus I was able to verify the modifications in the normal temperature of an organism affected by love.

Under pretexts that were often difficult to invent, I had the portrait returned to me for a few hours, noted the numbers and date, and set the thermometers again.

One evening when I'd danced twice with a little brunette, I recall having noted a drop in the temperature by four tenths, followed or preceded (there was no way to know the order of the phenomena) by a rise of seven tenths. These are the facts.

Be that as it may, once all was prepared, I took the following measures. I said to M. D***, "Property is theft" (it's not mine, it's not new, but it still works); to Mme D***, who had had a miscarriage that she talked about too often, "Women, from an economic and social standpoint, can and must be considered only as factories for fetuses"; and I sang, to the tune of "By a Crib," a few verses of a song by W*** called "By a Jar":

I saw him with his cord and caul,
A changeling, and a noble one!
If not for all that alcohol,
Just think of what he might have done!

Then I slipped a note into Virginie's hand:

"I'll explain everything later. Definitive quarrel between your parents and me. The ideal, the dream, the prism of the impossible, this is what awaits us. To live we must love . . . There's a carriage below: come, or I kill myself and you're damned."

That was how I abducted her.

The opportunities I'd encountered in this enterprise amazed me, when on the train I contemplated this young woman, raised peaceably, destined perhaps for some mediocre employee, who had followed me thanks to a series of sentimental formulas, which I hadn't invented, anyway, and which I couldn't really explain sufficiently.

We were going somewhere, supposedly.

In fact, long ago I'd prepared, with my personal sagacity, a delightful and methodical installation, whose goal will appear below.

We were on the train for three hours, plenty of time for dismay, sobs, and palpitations. Fortunately, we weren't alone in the compartment.

I'd previously studied, as much as possible, the situation in novels:

"You . . . You sacrifice everything for me . . . How can I acknowledge . . ." Then after a pause: "I love you, I love you . . . Oh, traveling with one's beloved! The horizon reddens at dusk, or in the morning is impearled with the dawn, and we are both face to face, after distraction or sleep, in lands of new perfumes."

I'd asked my friend the poet W*** to write that sentence for me.

We arrive, she like a wet bird, I delighted with the initial success of my research. For, without letting myself get carried away with the romantic conceit of *abduction*, during the voyage I had, all while comforting the poor frightened young woman, adroitly inserted between her tenth and eleventh rib a cardiograph of extended operation, so precise that Dr. Marey, to whom I owe its ideal description, had refused it on the grounds of economy.

Then a carriage met us at the station. Terror, embarrassment, and giddy anxiety from the young lady. My embraces, feebly rebuffed, permitted the cardiograph to record the visceral expressions of the situation.

And in the exquisite boudoir where, covering her eyes with her hands, she reproached herself for her definitive rupture with all the demands of morality and opinion, I was fortunately able to proceed to the exact measurement (the moment was of absolute importance) of the weight of her body. This is how I did it:

She had collapsed onto a sofa, lost in thought. Stopping, moved, delighted to contemplate her, I pressed with my heel the button of an electric bell hidden under the carpet, and, in the next room, in a secret office, on the end of a toggle lever whose other end was occupied by the sofa, Jean (my devoted and forewarned servant) could note the weight of the clothed young woman.

I threw myself beside her and lavished her with all possible consolations, caresses, kisses, massage, hypnotism, etc., consolations still not definitive, given my research plans.

I'll skip the transitions by which I made her drop her last pieces of clothing, still on the sofa, and then carried her into the alcove where she forgot family, opinion, and society.

During this time, Jean weighed the clothes left on the sofa, including the shoes and stockings, in order to obtain by subtraction the net weight of the woman's body.

Besides, in the room where, intoxicated with love, she abandoned herself to my fictional transports (for I didn't want to waste time), we were as if in a retort. The copper-lined walls prevented any contact with the atmosphere; and the air, first as it entered, and then as it left, was rigorously analyzed. The potassium solutions in the ball devices revealed to expert chemists, hour by hour, the quantitative presence of carbonic acid. I remember some curious numbers on the subject, but they lack the precision rightly demanded for the tables, since my respiration, which was not amorous, was mixed with Virginie's respiration, which really was. Let me simply mention, loosely speaking, the excess of carbonic acid released during those tumultuous nights in which passion attained maximum intensity and numerical expression.

Strips of litmus paper skillfully distributed in the lining of our clothes revealed to me the constantly acidic reaction of our sweat. Then in the following days, and following nights, how many numbers there were to record, on the mechanical equivalents of nervous contractions, on the quantity of tears shed, on the composition of saliva, on the variable hygroscopy of hair, on the tension of anxious sobs and sighs of pleasure!

The results of the *kiss counter* are particularly curious. The instrument, of my own invention, is no larger than those devices that puppeteers put in their mouths to make Punch speak, known as *swazzles*. Whenever the dialogue became tender and the situation appeared opportune, I put, secretly, of course, the device between my teeth.

Until then, I'd had only contempt for those expressions of "a thousand kisses" tacked onto the ends of love letters. That was, I told myself, only hyperbole passed into common language, quoting certain poets of dubious taste, like Johannes Secundus, for example. Well, I'm glad to provide experimental verification of those instinctive formulas that many scientists, before me, had considered absolutely fanciful. In the space of about an hour and a half, my counter registered *nine hundred and forty-four* kisses.

The instrument I'd put in my mouth bothered me; I was preoccupied with my research; and, besides, feigned actions never equal real ones. If you take all that into account, you'll see that this number of nine hundred and forty-four could often be surpassed by people who are violently in love.

This exquisite period of happiness for her, and fruitful study for me, lasted eighty-seven days. I'd established the series of decisive facts on which the *science of love* must necessarily be founded, except for the ninth and last part of my subdivision. This ninth part is entitled: *The effects of absence and sorrow.*

The study became delicate; fortunately, I could count on Jean (devoted servant) and on my faithful assistants, physicians, chemists, and naturalists.

"Virginie," I therefore said one morning, "blue dream of my life, star of my pallid future, I have forgotten in your arms some promissory notes that have been contested. I must therefore remove myself temporarily from the light of your eyes, from the magnetism of your kisses, from the dizziness of your embraces, and go wash this stain from my commercial life."

The scene she made confirmed what I'd already determined in a few preceding scenes concerning the *mechanism of sorrow.*

And I left, inflexible, not without leaving my assistants precise instructions so that they could take the last notes necessary for my memoir, whose academic impact promised to be devastating.

However, I was tired of all my patient research. When a chemist studies, with the greatest fervor, a kind of reaction, or general theory, he can at least, at mealtimes as well as at night, leave his laboratory and give his mind over to the ordinary events of life. The problem I was pursuing hadn't allowed me any time off. I had to be always ready for experiments; I had to shun all distractions and be constantly on the alert for the innumerable and complicated phenomena that arise in what is called an amorous intrigue.

Thus I took advantage of this respite from arduous work. Placing trust in my subordinates, I forgot for a moment, in low dancehalls, in recommended brothels, that uninterrupted intellectual tension that I'd undertaken so rigorously for the greater glory of science.

As I returned, on the train, I congratulated myself internally on the colossal work I'd accomplished. I told myself, rightfully, that my memoir would be a colossal beat on the gong for the scientific world, something like Newton's *Principia* or any other similar revelation.

My commendable persistence, I thought, as I rested on the cushions of the carriage that took me from the station to the villa, and the selflessness of such considerable expenditures, will finally earn their reward!

"Madame left three days ago," I was told, when I was back home.

"Left three days ago! It's not possible . . ."

"She left a letter for monsieur."

Here's the letter:

You would be contemptible, monsieur, if you weren't so stupid.

Oh, how bored I was at my parents after my studies at the Conservatory! You didn't understand how happy I was to find you to take me out of the paternal house. Thanks all the same, dear friend.

Jules W***, your friend, explained your plans to me.

You must be very young, without looking it, to think that this is what you learn from women.

By the way, I found all your instruments, all your registers. I was irritated (although you don't matter much to me!), and I broke everything, burned everything.

I even discovered the secret of the necklace you left me. Your thermometers, your hygrometers (that's the word, I think), all those informers, are in pieces.

And besides, what information could you have gotten from me about love? You always bored me to tears . . . Your friend Jules amused, and maybe even moved, me with his bohemian daring. You, never . . .

It was too sad in your boudoir filled with gadgets.

Adieu, my little scientist. I'm going to go stretch out my legs in the theater, abroad. A great Russian nobleman, less serious and more sensitive than you, is taking me away in his trunk.

VIRGINIE

All my dreams of glory destroyed, six hundred thousand francs (three-fourths of my fortune) a total loss, science delayed, on this subject, for several centuries: this was the picture that passed through my mind as I read the letter. Not wanting to believe it, I searched the villa from cellar to attic.

Appalling disaster! Everything, in fact, was broken, ground under the heels of her boots; charred documents floated here and there like a swarm of black butterflies.

And, as a last laugh from fate, I felt, as I walked through those empty rooms, among the ruins of my future, I felt regret that Virginie had left! Yes, I missed that woman more than the best of my lost work! And I went off to swoon, O shame! by burying myself in the pillow, seeking the aroma of that hair that I must never touch again.

Worst of all, I lost the opportunity to record the analytical elements of such a profound heartbreak, of such a unique combination of violent sensations, because I forgot to attach the cardiograph!

AN INTERPLANETARY DRAMA
. . . .

La Esperanza, 24 August 2872

Ordinance cxvii from the 32nd Grand Master of Terrestrial Astronomy drew protests from the entire *Mocker Party*. Let us say it at once: this party, although it denies it fiercely, is strikingly similar to the *Freethinkers*, so much in favor a few centuries ago. It is so similar that one might fear seeing it carried to the same negative extremes, which would then require the same suppression.

The Mockers have called it a return to the onions of Egypt, to the shadows of the nineteenth and twentieth centuries; they have proclaimed it a restitution of the clergy of earlier times, a superstitious measure, a mythological fantasy introduced into that which is most essential for the proper functioning of modern human society.

I could easily reduce these empty complaints to nothing. First of all, it should be noted that the ordinance establishes nothing that has not already been in actual practice for many years. It does nothing but summarize what was stated in the individual regulations of virtually all terrestrial observatories, or in the conclusions of numerous decisions by the Supreme Court.

In fact, one would have to be unacquainted with the most elementary study of administrative law not to know the formalities required by all observatory councils for admittance to the great dome and the adjoining terrace; one must have read none of this century's astronomical journals to be unaware that even the name "mysteries" given to the dome and terrace, so criticized in the ordinance in question, is of common usage, and that certain long-standing official documents use it expressly.

It is the same for the special diet, for the obligatory celibacy for all astronomers who hope to progress beyond the fourth degree, for the vow demanded of them, and for the particular penalties to which they are subject, penalties that become more severe with higher degrees of offenders.

For a long time already, aspirants requesting admission to higher degrees have had to verify their state of celibacy and the austerity of their habits with proper documentation. Now, these things had become required in actuality some time ago, and Ordinance CXVII simply formalized a custom recognized as necessary from an ethical and political point of view. And in this, enactment of the ordinance, rather than narrowing the custom, made it broader and more equitable, foreseeing the abuse of certain overly stringent restrictions which were beginning to be introduced in many Astronomical Courts.

But I know that the Mockers will not be satisfied with these explanations. Custom, if you like, they will say, but bad and unjust custom, abuse of power, etc.

Concerning this last question, which also instantly proves the ignorance and thoughtlessness of those who raise it, I have no desire to enter into a debate, in the strict sense of the term. I shall confine myself to recounting an incident that will show, to even the most primitive minds, the necessity of vigorous regulations, like the ones that have prevailed naturally, and which have just been codified in Ordinance CXVII.

Perhaps one might recall the sudden unexplained retirement of a director of the Southern Andes Observatory, and the rumors that followed his retirement, some thirty years ago. There was talk of culpable negligence and violation of the "mysteries" of the dome. The very word "mysteries" appeared in the newspapers of the time. The government wisely suppressed the affair; and the director, who was, moreover, missed for his extraordinary work, particularly on the equatorial fauna of Venus, had to retire for the sake of his health.

He died long ago, as have most of the interested parties. Here are the facts just as they occurred. I shall mention no names.

This director, unusually, even for that time, as I said above, had married. To tell the truth, he was a widower when he was nominated; but he still had a son of about twenty-two or twenty-three.

The young man, gifted with a vivid and almost un-disciplined imagination, had no taste for astronomical studies, and only wanted to make paintings and verses. Besides, he left poetry esteemed by specialists, although it has a bizarre character scarcely admissible for readers like myself, who appreciate only the normal incontest-able masterpieces of the twenty-fifth century. But let us return to our story.

The studies of Venusian flora were done by exchange, as is usually done; that is, as many types of Earthly flora had to be transmitted as were received from Venus. For this purpose, they used the great combination of three thousand fifty-centimeter lenses, with the correspond-ing reflectors. As is known, this telescope, which resem-bles the eye of an enormous insect, and which cost the builders twenty-nine years of work and the government ninety-five million, is still one of the finest telescopes on Earth. Images are reproduced at four hundredths of their diameter for the distance from Earth to Venus; so that Venusian astronomers need only enlarge the images four hundred times on the transmission surface for us to re-ceive them at their actual size.

They proceeded then to the exchange of Venu-sian and Earthly botanical types, keeping the telescope trained constantly on a mountain on Venus, which there is no need to specify. The director, engrossed in the ab-sorbing demands of his research, had the idea, more un-fortunate than culpable, of asking his son to assist him in the fixing and classification of the photographs transmitted to him.

Later, he went so far as to entrust the young man with the post of direct observer at the eyepiece. This can be explained only by a kind of senile dementia; for, during the inquiry, as justification for such a serious breach of metaplanetary agreement, the unfortunate director simply cited "fatigue of his eyes" at the time. But let us continue.

The great botanical research occupied half the time of the transmission; the other half was devoted to routine correspondence. The young man was thus instructed in all the procedures of this correspondence, but without study, without the diet, without degrees or vows!

The subordinate astronomers, perhaps more concerned with collecting their salaries than with watching over social matters, or even more because of their habit, commendable for that matter, of obedience and absolute respect for their director, these astronomers did not interfere. In addition, as they said in the inquiry, the correspondence service was conducted, under those irregular conditions, in a very active and prolific manner.

I shall call the young man, simply to facilitate the story, by the very common and banal name of Glaux.

Glaux, then, seemed to have immediately taken his observational duties very much to heart. He investigated every possible improvement he could bring to the transmissions. It was even he who first put into practice many methods previously dismissed as purely theoretical and inapplicable.

It was not, in fact, until these events that it became possible to transmit and receive auditory phenomena. The utility of this was denied; it was said that we understand very little about Venusian music, and that we can only speak the languages through the mechanical articulator. Speaking them, it was added, would be a waste of our time, except in the obviously absurd supposition of an interplanetary voyage.

This, in my opinion, was a quite hasty and pessimistic conclusion. I shall continue.

What was the reason for his sudden astronomical zeal? The cause would have been easy to predict, if old routine had not led most men to view the most natural things in the world as strange or impossible. Truly, science has progressed more rapidly than reason and common sense.

This is what happened.

Glaux, having finished his routine correspondence one day, was about to quit his post when he saw on the terrace of the Venusian observatory a being he did not recognize as part of the personnel up there.

Acknowledging in advance that I understand the scientific distinctions and restrictions, I shall say, to cut things short, that she was a *woman*.

Here my task as narrator becomes difficult. It would be impossible if Ordinance cxvii had not precisely defined violations of the press law. I shall therefore stay strictly within the law, and I shall be prudent about the details.

She was, therefore, a woman. Glaux, his curiosity aroused, observed her movements. She moved lazily, here and there. I can say nothing about her *extraterrestrial* beauty, or her adornments, of which our most sumptuous flowers could give only a drab and monotonous suggestion ... Only sworn astronomers of the eleventh degree can be informed precisely about these matters, and by other means than a description made of words.

But then She approaches the apparatus of Earthly correspondence and halts there.

Glaux gives her the usual greeting to initiate correspondence. She responds very appropriately, suppressing what one might call, in a legitimate analogy, a *burst of laughter*.

These details are taken from the journal in prose and verse left by Glaux.

Once they exchange a few signs, Glaux sees with surprise that She is, perhaps more so than he, familiar with the interplanetary language, and the dialogue continues.

But Earth and Venus turn; atmospheric refractions blur the images, soon permitting nothing more than the signs, repeated many times: Until tomorrow!

It was after this that Glaux was seen to put so much zeal and ingenuity into his duties as correspondent.

Did he himself invent those marvelous methods that we no longer think of admiring, now that they are in constant use, or did he receive some communication about them? Perhaps there had already been indiscretions, very advantageous for us, on the part of the young Venusian, unconcerned, as women generally are, with keeping the scientific secrets of her planet.

The reader has already guessed: the two young people had fallen in love. What madness! What a deplorable result of not observing regulations!

They tried to overcome the distance that separated them by exchanging complete records of their bodies. They sent each other their photographs, in series sufficient for replicating three dimensions and movement.

Glaux, in those hours when the observatory was closed, locked himself in a room and reproduced in smoke or dust the moving image of his beloved, an impalpable image made of light alone. He also realized her immobile form in malleable substances.

It was then that he thought of sending each other the sounds of their voices, their words, their songs. All of these were notated by curved lines and reproduced by the electrical pitch apparatus. I can say nothing about the words and songs (?) that arrived from so far away.

Everything that I have just told so briefly, and with good reason, lasted three years.

The third year was terrible, a mixture of rapture and despair ... Could those two fools have been saved, at that moment, by energetic means? It is doubtful. The harm had been done, irreparably.

One evening when our twilight corresponded to twilight in the Venusian area in question, and all preparations had been made on both sides, Glaux and the young woman exchanged a last kiss across implacable space and killed themselves.

This catastrophe almost compromised the good relations between the two planets, for the young Venusian was the daughter of one of the most powerful astronomers up there.

Everything was settled by the precise metaplanetary agreements that were then concluded. Ordinance CXVII sanctioned those agreements on Earth. This avoided the unfortunate aftermath that might have been feared at the time.

All of Glaux's papers, photographs, photosculptures, and phonographs have been placed in the central archives. One must, as I said, have attained the eleventh degree to gain access to them.

Despite all that I have just recounted, and by superior authorization as well, I do not despair of seeing the Mockers continue to deny the expedience of Ordinance CXVII.

THE NEWSPAPER OF THE FUTURE
. . . .

I arrived at the offices of the *Chat Noir* and was so over-whelmed by the Asiatic opulence of its salons that, roll-ing my hat between my fingers, I stood for two hours in a hallway bustling with a thousand busy employees, all wearing the most polymorphic and polychromatic uniforms.

I was pushed into a waiting room. The draperies, the divans, the incense that burned in the corners redoubled my timidity.

However, defeated by fatigue and emotion, and not daring to let myself sink onto the soft ottomans that cluttered the editorial salons, I noticed a little cane stool with *three* legs and sat on that, thinking myself hardly worthy.

Immediately a strange dizziness overtook me: M. Grévy appeared in the guise of Jupiter, chaser of nymphs; Salis held a lyre like Apollo and, smiling myste-riously, sang to me:

This tripod turns the least divine
Of mortal spirits sibylline.

In fact, the walls seemed to move away, the ceilings became domes of tropical greenery, the late winter flies multiplied in the form of chirping hummingbirds.

The wall calendar (from which one tears a sheet every day) lit up with an electric flash, revealing the fatal date: 1 March 1986.

"Why a 9 instead of an 8?"

"It's quite simple," whispered Rodolphe, "we're a hundred years older."

"But then, we're going to die?"

"Don't try to be funny. You know very well that ever since that invention by the famous American Tadblagson, our brains have been cast in platinum by electroplating; and that, when they're used up, we receive identical copies, since the molds are kept and catalogued at City Hall."

"And where are we?"

"In the offices of the *Chat Noir.*"

In fact, around an enormous emerald table, sit the writers. They're not handsome, these writers; they have faces like moving men; they're all dressed in gray canvas, with serial numbers on their collars. Each wears a sort of hat, shaped like a pumpkin, connected to his forehead with a series of keys, like the device hatters use to take their measurements.

The clock strikes five.

The ten writers at the end clap telephones to their left ears, and with their right hands write on a continuous strip of paper, which a machine unrolls before them. As soon as the paper is covered with writing, it's pulled through a slot, into the basement where the printing office is.

Alphonse Allais, as an obliging guide, explained things to me:

"These are the reporters of the news; the telephones tell them what's happening everywhere, and they write it down with the talent they draw from those singular hats.

"I almost forgot to tell you that those hats contain metallic brains, the finest models complete with batteries and accessories. The points touching the foreheads transmit the electric current, which produces talent in the most obtuse heads.

"This invention, due to the famous Tadblagson, transformed the social order by making talent proportional to wealth. That's why the greatest genius of our time is the banker Philipfill, who was able to afford the luxury of collecting the most expensive brains. Among others, it's said that he paid a million and a half for the brain of Sarah Bernhardt, guaranteed accurate.

"The result is that we've finished with all the socialist demands of the last century. Now the axiom is: no money, no talent. There are rare exceptions of penniless people born with intelligence; but our courts promptly intervene and expropriate their brains, returning all the models to the State.

"The *Chat Noir* of 1986, which wants to interest its readers at all costs, has made the greatest sacrifices to enrich its cerebral collection. So, the ten principal writers, two of whom write in verse, wear five million on each of their heads. The one on the left has a Victor Hugo brain. Besides, let's take a look. Ten after five ... he's already written two hundred verses, twenty a minute."

I lean over eagerly to read a few verses; the paper unrolled so quickly that this was all I could read:

. . . .

The rugged sandstone disk drives water from the furrow,
The blade of tempered steel must whistle, hiss, and glint,
The steel must acquiesce before the biting flint,
And at that fatal touch, its sparks must be acuter
Than those in women's eyes when yielding to a suitor.

. . . .

"Oh, that will probably be cut in the editing. The wearer's brain has some influence, sometimes too much, on his work. This one's a knife-grinder and he put in some things about his own job.

"We take, as you see, our writers from the humblest classes; they're more reliable, less expensive, and put less of their own qualities into their work.

"Sometimes, to obtain unexpected effects, we combine two or three different brains. For example, look at this writer bent double under two stacked hats. He wears, in addition to his own brain (which has little effect), that of Théodore de Banville, the poet, combined with that of a lawyer known to some scholars.

CHARLES CROS

"With my scissors, I'll cut out what he's just written—he won't notice—and you can judge the effect."

This is what was on the paper:

. . . .

One night I had her, there's no sense in giving
More detail.
Her pale and common parents made a living
In retail.

My heart, despite her horror at such crudeness,
Was broken . . .
But none, said Cujas, charging it with lewdness
Had spoken.

Who gazed at her, beneath her shiny makeup,
Profoundly?
The question's one my heart will gladly take up,
And roundly.

I said; you'll get no jewels all aglitter;
I'll lay out
No diamond, ruby, franc, or pint of bitter:
No payout!

What if her body lost, as I so judge it,
Its talents?
I'd be more prudent if I kept my budget
In balance!

. . . .

"This evening, it doesn't make any sense; but sometimes it surprises the reader.

"Five fifteen ... Stop! The copy's finished. All the writers lay down their pens and telephones. They return their hats to the numbered compartments and leave, as stupid as they were before they put them on, and collect three and a half francs from the cashier.

"The writing of the paper is nothing, as an expense, compared to the cost of the administrative staff and the equipment.

"The equipment? I'm not surprised it would be expensive. Imagine enormous greenhouses, filled with palm trees and orchids, buzzing with sunbirds and hummingbirds! The hummingbirds are even annoying.

"Fortunately, the American Humbugson has just invented a powdered hummingbirdicide.

"And the walls that seem so distant, over there, and those jagged rocks, are made of aggregate concrete, luminous at night.

"I won't describe the basement printing office, where no printing is done, because young ladies with exquisite voices dictate the copy onto phonographs, which, reproduced in millions of copies, bring the *spoken* paper to subscribers.

"Nobody knows how to read or write anymore—that's progress!—because of the phonograph. You can find only a few people who are old-fashioned like those among the dregs of humanity—they're the ones hired as writers . . ."

Crack! My *three*-legged cane stool broke under my contortions.

And I fall back into our own sad era, into the offices of a paper in 1886.

What a miserable facility you have nowadays, my poor *Chat Noir*!

THE STONE WHO DIED OF LOVE

....

(Story Fallen from the Moon)

On the 24th of Tchoum-Tchoum (comput of Vega, 7th series), an appalling moonquake devastated the Sea of Tranquility. Horrible or charming fissures appeared in the virgin* but infertile soil.

A piece of flint (there was no chipped stone then, and even less a possibility of polished stone) risked rolling down an isolated mountain peak and, proud of his rotundity, settled down about a *phthwfg*† from fissure A. B. 33, commonly called Monkey-Mold.

The pinkish look of the area, all new to him, a piece of flint just arrived from his mountain peak, and the black foam of magnesium that overhung the cool abyss,

---

* We take no notice of the vile slander that has circulated about this soil.

† The *phthwfg* equals a length of 37,000 meters of iridium at 7 degrees below zero.

panicked the bold stone, who stopped—hard, upright, and stupid.

The fissure burst into a delicious laugh, but a silent one, characteristic of that airless planet's beings. Her features, in this laugh, far from losing their grace, gained an indefinable quality of exquisite modernity. Wider, but more coquettish, she seemed to say to the stone, "Come on, then, if you dare! . . ."

The latter (whose real name was *Skkjro**) decided to prelude his amorous assault with an aubade, sung in the void redolent with magnetic oxide.

He used the imaginary coefficients of an equation of the fourth degree.† It is known that in ethereal space one obtains in this way incomparable fugues (Plato, Book XV, §13).

The fissure (her lunar name means "Augustine") at first seemed receptive to this homage. She even weakened, welcoming.

The Stone, emboldened, started to take advantage of the situation and roll farther, maybe penetrate . . .

Here the drama began, a drama that was brief, brutal, and true.

---

* This name, common on the Moon, translates exactly as "Alfred."
† The original lunar text reads "of the landing on the fourth floor." An obvious copyist's error.

CHARLES CROS

A second moonquake, jealous of this idyll, shook the dry ground.

The frightened fissure (Augustine) closed up forever, and the stone (Alfred) exploded in rage and cashed in his chips.

It is from this time that we date the age of *Chipped Stone*.

SMOKY DIAMOND

. . . .

Mad to begin with. And I exerted all my power to return her to real life. I didn't want to love her, I didn't love her; but later I grew attached to her as to a personal project.

Her madness was turbulent, talkative, anxious. I had to expend enormous energy to follow and tame this madness. Exaggerated, frightening speed in the movements of her thoughts; and moreover, a stock of fictional impressions of Parisian life, of journalism, of backstage gossip. And with it a feeling inherent in her being—all women have it, more or less—the overwhelming desire to impress people, almost without caring if the impression were true. To be known, for good or bad, what difference did it make! Publicity, publicity. That was even the source of all the wrong she did to me.

So, seduced by the picturesque but unhealthy depths of her disordered soul, I won her confidence and that of her entourage. I took care of her. I saved her from extreme measures, from the isolation that would have killed her, by promising, against the opinion of the authorities, that she could be cured. It came to be. But my energetic behavior, my deliberate and necessary coldness, had offended her self-esteem as a woman. And she used the forces she'd regained to subjugate me, to make herself loved.

Many times, I was seated next to her, and, as if succumbing to fatigue, she laid her head on my shoulder. I didn't want that. But I felt myself caught; I felt her persist; I knew where inexorable love was leading us.

Once, in a carriage, after I don't know what words I'd said—had there been some involuntary vow in those words?—she asked: "So, you love me?" And violently, driven by an irresistible internal storm, I answered her by pressing my lips to hers.

She's the type who doesn't attract me at first, but whom fate brings close to me, and from whom I suffer.

After that, domination, tyranny. She ordered me to dream of this or that, to write such and such a kind of poem. Hence my sterilization. I escaped by surrendering that which didn't matter to me—and a woman sees nothing but that.

And then, my obsession over what she said about every word, about every caress. I loved her, though; for I'd succeeded in awakening within her a delightful basic nature, hidden by all the plastering of fiction. I'd succeeded by making myself naive and primitive—it appears that I really am—and by persisting in seeing in her only the eternal virgin, the unbroken flower.

I was wrong to do this, perhaps; I knew enough not to believe in her purity. But I have no regrets. In fact, my dream had transformed and beautified her. My naiveté charmed her, and, not wanting to trouble it, she put herself in unison with me.

Then, sometimes, even more naive than I, she thought she was sampling me as a connoisseur. I pretended not to notice.

She complained at first about her lack of influence over me, reproaching me for former loves and possible dreams. I made her do everything, she claimed, without ever saying "I want." She sensed something unchanged in me, beneath my appearance of absolute and exaggerated obedience. It grew, and she became my intellectual enemy. But her body and soul—if not her mind—were mine. Painful period, however. I dreamed at times of distance and freedom.

But our souls were and will always be in agreement; my lassitude was all physical. I thought that perhaps she felt the same, and I insisted that she take her usual summer vacation. I had to remain in Paris; knowing this, she consented to leave without me.

Then there were a couple of those fateful occurrences that are never put into novels but are found in all stories that are true.

I don't justify myself; I was wrong, because our story was like a naive and pure novel. But the earlier irritation, the fatigue she and her entourage had instilled in me! She shouldn't have demanded the vow that I refused to give, in my horror of the false and in my hope of atoning by her momentary coldness or mistreatment—harsh punishments for me!—for what I'd done wrong on my part.

She did it, looking for reasons to keep me distant despite subsequent reconciliation, so that she could act badly more freely. For I found that she added to her resentment her interest in *impressing people*. Citing the law of an eye for an eye, she sold her smiles, for the dishonest prestige of signing someone else's work. And she was still attached to me, since she'd never said, "It's over."

If she'd loved the buyer, I'd have accepted the change of fate, I'd have bowed my head and bid her adieu. But she loved me; she loves me still, as I love her; she loved me still because she hid from me to sell herself. Her madness was horrible; I fled, cursing her.

Then, I wanted to crush the defiler of the dream, hoping I'd hurt myself in my revenge. Her vanity would have been satisfied with a semblance of drama, even a real drama. And with pretended partialities to make me angrier. I acted, but I saw everything. I saw that she still loved me, and I was even more upset, more amazed at her madness. I acted, because he deserved it. He ran away; he collapsed without the resistance my rage demanded.

Oh, the horror of my soul at the time! This is the draft of a letter to her (I never wrote her):

"You preferred deceitful prestige (and what prestige!) to purity, to justice, to love. You are cursed, you are damned. Keep your heart empty. As for me, I shall never return. Your behavior is so vulgar, so ugly, that it even took from me those failures of reason, those vague desires one always has to return to a former love. I would see in you the one who was never what I had believed.

"To prefer the inept joy of managing to pass for something you aren't to the sacred intoxications of love, this is common insanity, this is the immorality of the crossroads.

"I don't regret you; for you've never really been in love with me. I was mistaken. I don't hate you; I pity you."

Thus my terrifying sorrow turned to rage and insults. Yet if she'd called me back, held out her arms ... at certain dark hours, yes, I would have obeyed, like a madman, like a drunk; but at other moments, no! No! She'd behaved too badly.

Then months, months. All was dark; all hope closed off, all expansion stifled in my breast. Waking up to imagine some abject reunion, I was as cowardly inside as I was proud on the outside. Enormous desire to see her again, immobilized in a pride of granite.

One evening, I was double. Go forward or go back, toward her or away from her. Two urges that were frightening and *equal*. For a long time, I remained immobile, pulled by these two monsters. Horrible suffering that left traces in the physical condition of my heart. Finally, an intermediate goal appeared, and I ran after it. The night was spent in acts of madness that charmed two random women.

And then long afterward, I wrote this, which I kept in a notebook that I now find (I wrote to heal myself).

My most lucid self was elsewhere, during this ending. I'd been driven by the vague instinct to imitate what was usually done, and not by correct thought. I had no desire to deceive anyone, since I thought I was acting according to my true nature. This kind of weakness came from external facts, long expected, but against which my heart revolted.

No, the actions of a person cannot change my feelings toward her, I see her and accept her as she is, and her actions are a consequence of who she is.

She'd been treacherous, deceitful, and wicked; she'd childishly compromised the harmony between our souls for low temporal interests. I'd loved her for what was best in her, while knowing everything that was possible, since I knew she'd already profaned love by simulating it, in order to profit (she believed) from the brilliance of those she approached. This is wrong, according to those who judge actions isolated from people.

She simulated love, but she deceived herself first; which resulted in more madness, but less ugliness. I knew that, and I loved her anyway. She began again, at my expense; she frightened me off; I ran away, but I still love her. For it's all of her, with her lights and shadows, that I love.

My flight then had only one meaning: she'd given me all she could of true and faithful love, and then I saw

that it was over. There was nothing there I hadn't expected. But the broken happiness made me lose my sense of
the real, for there was reproach and anger in my flight.
Fortunately, that was all there was; I'd be afraid to find
myself in days like that again.

Why do I love her so? She's not a brilliant mistress,
since mad nights and voluptuous abandon frighten her,
since she's not completely a woman. Is it that state of the
eternal virgin, the seductive statue that the defilements
of satyromaniacs cannot penetrate?

She said, however, that she detested my dreams,
my works, my friends. To me, everything she pursued
seemed childish, empty, or unhealthy. She wasn't the
type that immediately charms me. I was told she wasn't
beautiful. Her face is faded from worldly troubles, the
fatigue of supplications, and clumsily used cosmetics;
her lips are withered and chapped from mad fevers. And
most of the things she does or says have always irritated
me beyond endurance, since they're just performances,
repetitions, of what she read in borrowed books, saw in
the theater or at famous people's houses, which her vanity makes her frequent without distinction.

So, few pleasures between us; often quarrels. But, at
delicious moments, we gazed into each other's eyes, con-
templating our souls.

At the beginning, she was wrong to make me leave my
mistress; at the end, I was wrong to show myself jealous of
her flesh. But freedom from those things is only a dream.

Now the situation is sad, very sad. Without counting the terrible suffering I've endured since that last day until a time not too long ago, whenever we see each other, we're caught in a painful lie. She lives with indifferent people, gaily talks about everything to one person or another. Me, I do the same, I try to shake off my stupor by taking, in pursuit of fun and excitement, some woman I shouldn't even notice before her.

But given what we'd been to each other, we speak only rarely, and with some embarrassment. Our voices take on a false sharpness, since our natural tones would let our trembling be heard. It's all very painful, and I see no end to it.

I love her soul and I'm sure she loves mine. I've dreamed of insane transactions to propose to her. I would like her to be my sister; for my only desire would be to see her often and to look deeply into her eyes, with no cause for trouble between us.

I thought: Why our deceitful attitudes? We found ourselves alone, and we no longer spoke as we used to. When I see her, I'll say, "Do you remember?" She'll answer yes, and I'll continue, "Then—to begin with, I might fear your cold and haughty refusal—throw your arms around my neck and press your lips to mine. To do anything else would be dishonest. We've been more than brother and sister. And one never stops being brother and sister."

It was a plan I never carried out.

I've seen her again, however, and often. She read my verses that spoke of her: I myself read her those verses in which I castigated her, others in which I remembered her sadly, and others in which I expressed my weary resentment. I was frank only in my verses, and after reading them, I became, despite myself, falsely exuberant and distracted, or sad for external reasons.

One evening, she signaled to me with her eyes (like before) to come sit by her. It was the first time, in two years, that something from the past was really repeated between us. I obeyed, and asked her, "Is this a bet?" She told me, reproachfully, no; then she talked about my verses. Then our chat, almost at full voice before the talkative diners, turned to the past, to our final catastrophe. Blaming fate and me, somewhat, she wanted to justify herself. "Why defend yourself? Since I return here, I have no contempt for you that you need to get rid of." She continued; but I said, "No, you acted badly. If I deserved it, you should have told me you were leaving me before doing it." But she continued, and I, still, "I don't blame you for anything; I loved you with all your perversity; I didn't want to change you; but you acted badly."

Since then, she's had no hostile words or looks for me. I think both of us dream of starting again as we were before, but without enough resolution for it ever to happen.

THE SONG OF THE MOST BEAUTIFUL WOMAN
. . . .

I am the most beautiful of all women who existed before me, who live now, and who will be born after.

I play musical instruments marvelously. My voice has marine depths and celestial heights. The words that I speak have never been heard before.

The harmonies because the strings are brushed by my white fingers, the songs because they come from my dazzling mouth, the words because my all-powerful gaze floats above them, are words, songs, and harmonies that are eternal.

I am the most beautiful of women, and my greatest joy is to be seen, to be loved, above all by him who took me, but also by those who are beneath him.

All furs taken from the rarest wild beasts, all the fine linen and silk that men make, all of it is brought to me and I stretch out on it, and my beautiful white body shivers on those soft riches with their subtle aromas.

For strong men, for him who conquered so many other men to possess me, the harsh fatigues of the hunt and war;

Me, I enjoy well-tended gardens, small, perfumed rooms, draped with beautiful soft fabrics, strewn with cushions.

I am beautiful and strong, but I am a woman, and I enjoy the comforts that also appeal to men who are weak and sick,

Warm interiors, filled with glittering flowers,

Palanquins for traveling, or even the shoulders of maidservants to support me when I drag the folds of my robe carelessly through well-tended gardens.

I am beautiful and strong, I give birth without suffering and my body remains pure and smooth. It is a calm and slow pleasure for me to hold my pink child in my arms and to feel his little mouth suck the tip of my solid breast, while his eyes laugh and seem to respond to my smile. It is a calm and slow pleasure equal to the tumultuous pleasure felt under a lover's caresses.

I feel my blood rise to my breast and become the warm milk that feeds my pink child and makes him grow.

Two of my white fingers press the tip of my solid breast so that it stands out and so that my child, as he sucks me, can look at me with his laughing eyes and thus respond to my smile of delight.

I am delighted to feel my own substance pass into him; I feel my blood rise to my breast and become the warm milk that serves to form the body of my child, so pink and so excellent to kiss.

I am beautiful and strong; I gave birth without pain and my body remained pure and smooth.

My lover finds my solid breasts more appealing since they have fed my pink child; I am no longer, he says, a budding flower with the scent of greenery, but from now on a blooming flower with the heady scent of ambergris.

My child is big enough to play among the maid-servants and to cause naive terror with his prophetic boldness.

I am beautiful and strong, I gave birth without pain to a bold child, and I became more attractive to my lover, because of my smooth and voluptuous body.

I am the most beautiful of women, and when I appeared before the eyes of men, all wanted to have me.

Thus great discords and great disasters. I have some-times wept in the name of those who died for me, for among them were proud gazes and high souls that I could well have loved.

And yet I was happy when the handsomest of all, he who had the most powerful gaze, since he was the final victor, came to ask for my soul and my body.

I gave him my soul and my body, happy that fate had chosen him for me in those combats where so many others had fallen, among whom I might perhaps have hesitated.

When I stretch out on the cushions, folding my arms over my head, the attraction of my bright gaze, of my solid breasts, of my snowy thighs, of my heavy hips, is all powerful.

It is for this that so many men have been captivated, that so many men have killed one another.

And he who took me is entirely possessed by the attraction of my bright eyes that will shine with eternal poems, is subjugated by the abandon of my solid breasts, of my snowy thighs, and of my heavy hips. He feels, in these curves that I give to him, the charm of absolute beauty and the creative will that makes my body the source of the noblest races of the future.

PEOPLE OF LETTERS
. . . .

I

Once upon a time there were a king and a queen, who
were very upset that they had no children.

The king, who was called His Majesty O, said to the
queen, who was called Her Majesty E:

"Heaven has not blessed our union; we must consult
your godmother, the fairy Spider."

King O had a big belly. When he slapped it, it went
tock, tock. Queen E had no belly at all, she was lean, like
a salt herring. And the children didn't come.

They telegraphed the fairy Spider, who came down
the chimney with three fat cabbages that she put in a pot
right away, and good bacon, and salt, and pepper . . . And
then she made a lot of soup (there was quite enough for a
hundred people) and gave it to Queen E to eat. Cabbage
soup made by a fairy is fairy soup. That is why Queen E,
so lean at first, swelled, swelled, swelled. And the next
morning they found, in three cradles, the first draped in
gooseberry satin, the second draped in buttercup satin,
and the third draped in satin the color of a cloudless sky,

three little princesses, who were more beautiful than the stars, the sun, and the moon.

The fairy Spider, who was from the famous Aiou family, so renowned in the fabric business, cut her name in three and called her first goddaughter A, her second I, and her third OU.

II

The three princesses became even more beautiful as they grew.

It was charming to see them run under the foliage, whistling at blackbirds, running after butterflies, picking fresh hazelnuts.

One evening King O said to Queen E:

"We must marry off our daughters, the beautiful princesses A, I, and OU. We'll have some trouble with Princess A, since she's like a goose, she honks at all the gentlemen and all the ladies at court. Princess I will be easier, she laughs all the time; we'll give her to some scatterbrained prince. As for the third, little OU, it will happen without us; she's always afraid, she wants to run away to the woods, but she's as cute as a button."

The queen said to the king:

"Let Your Majesty not forget that our three princesses have only one (very thin) chemise between them, a gift from their godmother, the fairy Spider. The people are crushed by taxes, and the tobacconists will never earn us enough to buy them more chemises."

King O said:

"Oh!"

Boom, boom, boom! What's that? A cannon! Ah! It's a visit from next door. Is it the King of Under-the-counter, the neighbor? No, it's his three sons, Prince P, Prince T, and Prince K.

"Well now, wifey mine, maybe there's a way to place our three princesses . . . Hey, I'm talking to you, Queen E, E, E. Are you asleep?"

"Sire, marry them off as you like."

(Boom, boom!) "Get up, sire, and let's go sit on our thrones, to receive the princes."

It must be said that King X of Under-the-counter was no richer than King O. He had asked the Wizard Merlin to be the godfather of a son, promised to him by Queen Z. But when Merlin came to the baptism, he saw that instead of one son, Queen Z had three, who were named Prince P, Prince T, and Prince K, as you know.

But the Wizard Merlin, counting on only one godson, had prepared only one gift. It was a magic sword with a sapphire hilt. Even the greatest wizards cannot change their decisions. So Merlin said to King X:

"Too bad! My godsons will have only one sword for the three of them."

It was not stinginess that moved Merlin, for with his magic he brought down falling stars that became chocolates, sugared almonds, and twenty-sou coins.

Prince P became an eater, Prince T became a dancer, Prince K became a hunter.

III

Boom! Boom! King O and Queen E are sitting on their thrones.

Prince P comes forward and says:

"Oh, King O, will you give me your daughter, Princess A, in marriage?"

Queen E says to King O:

"He's a glutton, he eats a lot, he eats too much, but that will suit our daughter A. Give her to him."

King O says:

"Prince P, I give you my daughter A."

Then Prince T comes forward and asks to marry Princess I who was doubled over in laughter, and Prince K asks for the hand of Princess OU, who was hiding behind the sideboard, but was content all the same.

The three weddings took place the next day, to the sound of fifes and drums. There were even bells that rang: do, ti, la, do, ti, la. They distributed fried potatoes, radishes, and cider to the enormous crowd, who blessed the king, the queen, and the three young couples.

The king, a tear in his eye, gave a kingdom (while reserving his rights to common walls) to each of his sons-in-law. In his paternal enthusiasm, he even went so far as to double their nobility.

So Prince P and Princess A, that made PA, they became the PAPA family, serious people who eat a lot; likewise Prince T and Princess I formed the TITI family, people always dancing and laughing; and Prince K, with Princess OU, that makes KOUKOU, it's love, it's mysterious, it's in the woods. Cuckoo! Cuckoo!

IV

But in marriage, you need linens! And the godmother had given only one (and very light) chemise to her three goddaughters, as a wedding present. Oh, they all had their princess coats, embroidered with Oriental pearls, but underneath they had to wear the godmother's one chemise, and His Majesty King O was poor, although descended from an illustrious race.

So they made do all the same. The king gave a great ball for the weddings.

Princess A had the chemise.

After the first dance, at nine o'clock, she left to go to bed.

Prince P had the sword. He laid it on the night table, for fear of robbers and to show, in accordance with the law, that the husband must help and protect his wife.

At midnight the princess said:

"I've slept enough, let's go have dinner!"

And they returned to the ball. Princess A said to her sister Princess I:

"The chemise is rolled up in this bouquet of tea roses!'

Princess I left to go sleep in her room, having put on the (very light) chemise that smelled like tea roses.

Then Prince P said to Prince T:

"You'll find the sword in the anteroom, in the right corner. Don't forget the law."

Prince T found the sword and ran off to see if his wife was sleeping. She was sleeping. He put the sword next to the bed and fell asleep.

At three o'clock in the morning, Princess I woke up, smiling at the sight of the sword, and Prince T saw that she had a (very light) chemise. She said:

"I've slept enough, let's go dance! Let me get up and wait for me below."

And quickly she rolled up the chemise and put it in a bouquet of marjoram that was there for that reason. She put on her impearled coat and went downstairs.

When she entered the ball, she gave Princess OU, who was dancing her hundredth waltz, the bouquet of marjoram, saying:

"Go off quickly to bed, it's late; don't be afraid, your prince will follow you."

Oh! She was very afraid, was Princess OU; she would have preferred to run away. But the wood is all the way down there, so dark, and so wet!

Prince T said to Prince K:

"The sword is in the anteroom, in the right corner. Don't forget the law."

Princess OU was sleeping in her (very light) chemise when Prince K came into the room. He pulled the sword from the scabbard and fell asleep.

At six o'clock in the morning, Princess OU wakes up and says:

"I've slept enough. Let's go to the woods!"

V

Boom! Boom! Boom! It's not the celebration this time, or visitors; it's war.

The enemy attacks the kingdom from three sides at once.

Prince K jumps to the sword, Princess OU jumps from the bed, puts on her coat, and runs to the war with her prince. She's no longer afraid at all.

When they get to the wood, she picks eglantines and laurels.

Prince K runs to the right, runs to the left, runs straight ahead, and cuts off all the enemy's heads.

Prince P and Prince T would have liked to win the battle too. But without the sword—what to do?

The bells began ringing for the victory. The people all ran before the winner and his princess. Then they came back in proper order, loaded with the enemy's rich spoils.

There was gold, there was silver, by the millions. There were silk dresses, steel suits of armor. There were a hundred thousand cannons, just as many kegs of powder, and a hundred times as many shells. There were also kegs of wine, cider, and beer; no one counted the hams. There were also sixty thousand boxes of candied fruits, and many other things no longer known. But ... no linens; no swords!

VI

But here's the winners' chariot, decorated with eglantines and laurels. Prince K held in his hand three almost identical swords, and all three signed: Merlin. The sword with the sapphire hilt was the one he'd used to win the war. The two others, found in a colonel's old trunk (as if by chance, but it was really Merlin who'd prepared this surprise), the two others had, one a hilt of ruby, and the other a hilt of Oriental topaz.

Princess OU held on her knees a box of lapis lazuli latticed with gold, which contained two (very light) chemises, signed by the fairy Spider.

Prince K came down from the right side of the chariot and planted the three swords in the ground between him and his two brothers. He signaled the cannons: Boom! Boom! Boom! And the three princes, each raising a sword, saluted that happy day.

At the same time, on the left side of the chariot, Princess OU gave the box to her two sisters, whispering to them:

"There's one for each of you."

Princesses A and I understood they were chemises, and tenderly kissed their sister OU.

VII

After celebrations that lasted three months, they divided all the riches they'd won, and the three families, PAPA, TITI, and KOUKOU, took leave of King O and Queen E to go rule their own kingdoms. They were all very happy and had many children.

FANTASIES IN PROSE
. . . .

DISTRACTOR

The room is filled with fragrance. On the low table, in baskets, there are resedas, jasmines, and all kinds of little red, yellow, and blue flowers.

Blonde emigrants from the land of long twilights, from the land of dreams, the visions disembark into my imagination. They run, shout, and crowd so much, that I long to bring them out.

I take very white and very smooth sheets of paper, and amber-colored pens that glide across the paper with the cries of swallows. I want to give those restless visions the shelter of rhythm and rhyme.

But on the smooth white paper, where my pen glides crying like a swallow on a lake, drop flowers of resedas, jasmines, and other little red, yellow, and blue flowers.

It was *She*, whom I had not seen, who was jostling the baskets on the low table.

But the visions were still restless, still eager to leave. So, forgetting that *She* was there, lovely and white, I blew away the little flowers strewn across the paper, and returned to running after the visions, who, beneath their traveling cloaks, have treacherous wings.

I was about to imprison one—a wild girl with green eyes—in a narrow stanza,

When *She* came to lean on the low table, beside me, so close that her irritating breasts caressed the smooth paper.

The last line of the stanza remained to be sealed. Thus it was that *She* prevented me, and that the vision with green eyes escaped, leaving nothing in the gaping stanza but her traveling cloak and a little nacre from her wings.

Oh! The distractor!... I was about to give her the kiss she expected, when the shifting visions, those dear emigrants with their distant fragrance, renewed their dances in my imagination.

So, I forgot again that *She* was there, white and nude. I wanted to close the narrow stanza with a final line, an indestructible chain of ideal steel, nielloed with stellar gold, inlaid with the splendors of sunsets crystallized within my memory.

And with one hand I gently pushed aside her breasts, swollen with irritating desires, which hid the space for that last line on the smooth paper. My pen took flight again, crying like a swallow skimming a calm lake, before the storm.

But then *She* had stretched out, lovely, white, and nude, on the low table, underneath the baskets, hiding under her lovely languid body the entire sheet of smooth paper.

Then all the visions flew off, far away, never to return.

My eyes, my lips, and my hands were lost in the aromatic down of her neck, under the stubborn clasp of her arms, and on her breasts swollen with desires.

And I saw nothing more than that lovely body, so languid, warm, white, and smooth, on which dropped, from the jostled baskets, resedas, jasmines, and other little red, yellow, and blue flowers.

THE CABINET

To Madame Mauté de Fleurville

I needed very quick eyes, very sharp ears, very keen attention,

To discover the mystery of the cabinet, to go beyond the perspectives in the marquetry, to reach the imaginary world through the little mirrors.

But I finally glimpsed the clandestine party, I heard the minuscule minuets, I caught the complicated intrigues brewing in the cabinet.

You open the doors, you see a sort of salon for insects, you notice the white, brown, and black tiling in forced perspective.

A mirror in the center, a mirror to the right, a mirror to the left, like the doors in symmetrical comedies. In fact, these mirrors are doors opening onto the imaginary.

But an apparently unaccustomed solitude, a tidiness whose purpose eludes you, in this salon with nobody in it, an opulence pointless for an interior where only night would reign.

You're fooled by it, you say, "It's a cabinet, that's all," you think there's nothing behind the mirrors but the reflection of what is shown to them.

Insinuations that come from somewhere, lies whispered to our reason by deliberate policy, ignorance in which we are kept by certain interests, not mine to specify.

But I no longer want to be cautious, I scorn what might happen, I am not worried about fantastical grudges.

When the cabinet is closed, when the ears of intruders are stopped by sleep or filled with external sounds, when men's thoughts dwell on some concrete subject,

Then strange scenes occur in the cabinet's salon; characters of unusual size and appearance emerge from the little mirrors; certain groups, lit by vague lights, stir in those forced perspectives.

From the depths of the marquetry, from behind the simulated colonnades, from the ends of the false corridors depicted on the backs of the doors,

There come, in old-fashioned outfits, with a lively step, for an extraterrestrial almanac festival,

Dandies from an era of dream, young ladies seeking places in this society of reflections, and finally the elderly parents, stout diplomats and mottled dowagers.

On the polished wood wall, hung who knows how, the girandoles ignite. In the center of the room, hanging from a ceiling that does not exist, a chandelier sparkles, overladen with candles as pink, fat, and long as the horns of snails. In unexpected hearths, fires blaze like glowworms.

Who put those chairs there, as deep as hazelnut shells and set in a circle, those tables overladen with immaterial refreshments or microscopic bets, those sumptuous curtains—as heavy as spiderwebs?

But the ball begins. The orchestra, which one might think to be made up of cockchafers, throws out its evanescent notes, crackles, and whistles. Young couples clasp hands and bow to one another.

Perhaps even a few kisses of feigned love are stolen in secret, smiles void of thought hide behind fly-wing fans, faded flowers in corsages are asked for and given as tokens of reciprocal indifference.

How long will it last? What conversations arise in these parties? Where does this world without substance go, after the soirée?

No one knows.

Because, if you open the cabinet, the lights and fires go out; the guests, dandies, coquettes, and elderly parents disappear pell-mell, heedless of their dignity, into the mirrors, corridors, and colonnades; the chairs, tables, and curtains vanish.

And the salon remains empty, silent, and tidy;

Therefore everyone says, "It's a marquetry cabinet, and that's all," without suspecting that once they turn away,

Little mocking faces risk peeping from the symmetrical mirrors, from behind the encrusted columns, from the ends of the false corridors.

And you need a particularly practiced eye, both keen and careful, to surprise them when they retreat into those forced perspectives, when they seek refuge in the imaginary depths of the little mirrors, at the moment when they return to their unreal hiding places in the polished wood.

MADRIGAL
*translated from the back of a fan owned by Lady
Hamilton*

Time, that implacable alchemist, will deplete the sandalwood's warm perfume.

But these words on your fan will remain, and in them
you will still find the immaterial perfumes of memory.

Then the image of your radiant youth will unfurl within
your memory. You will be dazzled and delighted by it, as
we are dazzled and delighted when your copper hair un-
furls over your shoulders.

After that, time, delayed for a moment, will resume its
destructive work, and your flesh, that palpable dawn, will
instantly be carried off by the anger of fate or of man; or
it will slowly desiccate in the winds of age, to dissolve at
last into the brown earth.

This fan also, sold, bought, resold, soiled in dressers, broken by children, a curio scorned in junk shops, will finish

perhaps in a bright fire, or, shipwrecked in the sewers, float down rivers to crumble, rotten, in the enormous sea.

As you wait, keep the pride of your dawn-colored flesh, let your hair flame insolently, play with the perverse omnipotence of your transparent eyes.

For you are the current link in the perpetual chain of beauty; for that which shone once will shine forever in the absolute; for the symphony of your life needs a severe and grandiose final chord.

Besides, these words that speak of you, passed from memory to memory, will unceasingly revive the sovereign hand that held this fan, and the flesh that it caressed with every perfumed stroke.

ON THREE AQUATINTS

. . . .

by Henry Cros

I. *Dismay*

In the middle of the night, a dream. A railway station. Employees bearing cabalistic letters on their administrative caps. Openwork cars stocked with wrought iron demijohns. Ironclad wheelbarrows roll by with parcels that are loaded onto the cars of the train.

The voice of a deputy stationmaster cries, "Monsieur Igitur's sanity, headed for the moon!" A workman arrives and pastes a ticket on the designated parcel—a demijohn like those in the openwork cars. And, once weighed on the scales, it's loaded on the train. The departing whistle resounds, shrill, vertiginous, and prolonged.

Sudden awakening. The whistle ends in the mewing of an alley cat. Monsieur Igitur jumps up, shatters the window, and stares up at the deep blue, where floats the mocking face of the moon.

II. *Underwater Vanity*

Amphitrite, rosy and blonde, passes with her retinue at a murky distance, beneath the waters of the southern sea.

Like Parisian nymphs going to the woods, she herself drives her mussel shell, a delectable coach glazed in shining black, chased with azure and mother-of-pearl.

The beauty abandons her hair to the salted liquid breeze. Her eyes are half closed, and her pink nostrils dilate with pleasure in this adventurous race.

With what arrogance do her beautiful arms stretch out to hold the reins, thin green seaweed, of the spirited seahorses with their bright chestnut coats!

It is that surprising feminine absurdity, disastrous and adorable, prouder of the fabric she bought than of the white curves of her breast, vainer of the pedigree of her team than of the transparency of her pupils.

She is expected at some charity meeting where Nereids request donations, escorted in the middle of the crowd by Tritons starched into their ceremonial collars, and where Sirens must make themselves heard over the factories that produce the coral.

She will arrive late, somewhat on purpose, to make a sensational entrance in the middle of the official speech by Monsieur Proteus, a zealous organizer, but tiresome to listen to.

She will arrive late, because, happy to be watched, even by the humblest aquatic citizens, she will restrain her dashing seahorses and bridle them in place, pretending that she cannot urge them forward.

Besides, is it not charity to charm the eyes of so many poor people for free?

III. *The Piano-Ship*

The ship sails with dazzling speed over the ocean of imagination,

Driven by the vigorous efforts of the oarsmen, slaves of different imaginary races.

Imaginary, because their profiles are all unusual, because their bare torsos are colors that are rare or impossible in real races.

There are greens, blues, carmine reds, oranges, yellows, vermilions, as on Egyptian murals.

In the center of the ship is a raised platform, and on the platform a very long grand piano.

A woman, the Queen of Fictions, sits at the keyboard. Under her rosy fingers, the instrument yields velvety and powerful tones that muffle the whispering of the waves and the straining sighs of the oarsmen.

The ocean of imagination is tamed; no wave will be bold enough to spoil the piano's finish, a masterpiece of cabinetwork in gleaming rosewood, nor wet the felt of the hammers, nor rust the steel of the strings.

The symphony gives the route to the oarsmen and the helmsman.

But what route? And to what port does it lead? The oarsmen know nothing, nor the helmsman. But they continue, over the ocean of imagination, ever onward, ever more courageous.

Row onward, onward! The Queen of Fictions repeats it in her endless symphony. Every mile traveled is happiness gained, ever closer to the supreme and ineffable goal, even if it be unattainable infinity.

Onward, onward, onward!

THE COLD HOUR
. . . .

To Count Ferdinand de Strada

Evening twilights have left so many jewels in my memory that I need only speak the words "evening twilights, splendors of sunsets" to evoke both solemn recollections of earlier life and the raptures of intoxicated youth.

And then, after the twilight, soft transparent night, or even full night, as thick as fur.

Then, in Paris, the gas is lit. In the summer, the gas, shining through the trees in the gardens, gives the foliage, seen only from below, the dull green tint of fairy-tale scenery. In the winter, the gas in the fog recounts all the evening follies: tea and mulled wine in families, beer and clouds of tobacco smoke in cafés, orchestras that set awhirl, with their vibrant breath, the elegance of all classes,

Or the night of work: the lamp, the fireside, no noisy interruptions.

Then the shop windows go dark. Only official streetlamps have the right to cast their severe light.

Passersby become less frequent. People go home. Some look forward to the quiet bedroom, to the curtained bed (a good place to die); others miss the sporadic and deafening excitement of songs and cries in the open air. A few drunkards' quarrels.

Ladies in bonnets leave decent parties; sellers of pleasure whisper their prices, reduced due to the advanced hour.

You walk. You listen to your own footsteps. Everyone has gone home. Butchers, drowsy, receive enormous sides of beef, split and stiffened sheep.

Everyone is back home, selfishly and deeply asleep. Where to go? Every place of hospitality is shut. The fires are out. At best, you might find a few wisps of embers in the ashes of cooling hearths.

(In ancient life, this was the hour when those asleep at bacchanals are roused by their slaves. The dying lamps are refilled with oil. Drinks are served. The guests move. They sing. But it is only to forget the deathly influence lying over the house. Thus even the strongest are pale, bluish; uncontrollable shivers run through their bones.)

The transparencies of the night turn harsh or are veiled by mist. Oh! It is better to walk. Where to go? It is the cold hour.

Midnight is the fictitious astronomical border between the last day and the next. But the cold hour is the true human moment when another day will begin. At this hour the question seems to be raised, for every being, of whether the coming day will be added to those already lived, or whether the tally is now complete.

To be alone at home then, without sleeping, is horror. The angel of death seems to hover over all men, profiting from their implacable sleep to choose his prey when no one suspects.

Oh! Yes, at this hour, you could suffocate, you could groan, you could feel your heart burst and the bland tepid blood fill your throat, in a final spasm that no one would hear, for no one will leave the heavy dreamless sleep that keeps all earthly creatures from feeling the cold hour.

LASSITUDE

. . . .

For long periods in this short life, I try to gather my elusive thoughts, I seek visions of the good hours.

But I find that my soul is like a house deserted by the servants.

The master anxiously paces the cold halls, without the keys to the welcoming rooms that hold the wonders he brought back from so many voyages.

The moments of ecstasy, when I could hold the universe in my royal hand, were very brief and very rare. Almost as rare were my periods of normal thought. Most often I am powerless, I am mad; which I hide on the outside, under riches gained in the good hours.

What drug will give me normal thought more often? When I have it, when it lasts, my powerful chest permits me to rise beyond the reach of all earthly odors, up there where, in my ecstasy, I exercise my royalty.

After nights of poor sleep (where do they come from?), I am no longer up there. I can only miss what I felt there. I scarcely have the lucidity or the courage to tell other men what I did there or to justify myself to them.

I had every pride; I scorned all responsibilities and justifications.

But when dull fever has misled me and pulled me down, can I live alone, without sun, between walls of hatred?

And yet the efforts I consent to make, despite my lassitude, far from counting in my favor, do they not mark me instead for the fury of the restless crowds who rush below?

STUDY ON METHODS OF COMMUNICATION WITH OTHER PLANETS

. . . .

I

§1. I shall set out a project that will not be realized soon, I fear, because of the astonishment it provokes in most people. Its strangeness, however, is only superficial, for the elements are strictly scientific.

It concerns entering into communication with the planets closest to Earth, Mars and Venus, by means of luminous transmissions.

Obviously, once all other difficulties have been overcome, if there are no beings as intelligent as man on these worlds, the project will produce only negative results. But since its realization alone can settle the question, it is of great scientific interest, and it is rational.

The publicity I give it has no aim but to provoke discussion, and to indicate to astronomers a certain order of evidence that I find particularly interesting.

§2. Transmission between two planets is founded on the exchange of a repeated phenomenon, whatever that phenomenon might be.

In the current state of astronomical physics, we have no choice: we can only use a beam of light. Perhaps later it will be demonstrated that astral magnetism, electricity, or gravitation itself would be better, if these forces are applicable in this case.

§3. A free light, a candle for example, placed on an elevation, provides less light the farther we move away from it; and there is a distance at which we no longer see it. This is due to two causes. The first is that air is not absolutely transparent, and at a certain thickness acts like an opaque screen. The second is that light, since it expands equally in all directions, becomes more dispersed the farther it travels.

The relation between the quantity of light and the distance of the source is well known. A candle illuminates a sheet of paper placed a meter away; at a distance of two meters four candles are needed to produce the same illumination. At a hundred meters ten thousand candles would be needed; in short, a number proportional to the square of the distance.

Now, it is no longer by meters that we count the distance between planets, but by millions of kilometers. There is therefore no reason to hope that a free luminous focal point, intense enough to be seen in those distant worlds, could be produced and maintained by man. Calculations could easily prove this, but they are useless here.

§4. Faced with this insurmountable limit, we have no reason to despair of a solution to the problem; for optical physics will offer us unexpected resources.

The preceding discussion, in fact, concerns *free* light rays, that is, those expanding in all directions. Now, everyone knows that with an ordinary mirror, we can direct reflected rays at will. If therefore we imagine—returning to the example of the candle—arranging several mirrors around the flame, in such a way to send, to the same place, the rays reflected by each of them, this place will first receive the light coming directly from the candle, and in addition the rays reflected by the mirrors. Let us admit that each mirror sends one-fourth of the light it receives. The result will be that four mirrors will double the illumination; four hundred mirrors will multiply it by a hundred. It was by this method, it is said, that Archimedes used the heat of the sun to burn the enemy fleet.

Today, this collection of flat mirrors is replaced by a single concave mirror, whose curvature reflects all the rays, produced at the focal point, in the same direction. In this way, these rays, instead of dispersing in all directions, form themselves into a single beam, and the light travels through space without weakening save by reason of the opacity of the environment. Lenticular or graduated refractors have properties comparable to those of parabolic mirrors.

§5. This is how these facts will be applied to the transmission of interplanetary signals.

Since the source must be as intense as possible, electric light is clearly indicated. Let there be then a powerful electric lamp, placed at the focal point of a parabolic reflecting mirror whose principal axis is directed at the planet. The light rays that fall on the mirror are reflected parallel to the principal axis. The beam that they form is theoretically cylindrical; but in reality it is conical, for on one hand it is impossible to construct mirrors with rigorously exact curvatures, and on the other hand the luminous source is not a simple point that can coincide with the focal point. It follows that the rays will form a very elongated diverging beam, either as it leaves the mirror, or from the point at which this beam—assumed first to be convergent—is the most condensed. When this beam arrives at the planet, it will have widened enough to envelop the planet entirely, and to extend far beyond it as well. But the wider it is, the more its intensity will diminish.

Let us cut this beam with a white surface, normal to the axis, at the point where it is a meter in diameter. It is possible to give the electric lamp such an intensity that the surface will be, under these conditions, lit as brightly as by a ray of sunlight.

The beam is then assumed to widen as it travels through space; when it arrives at the planet it will be *twenty million* meters in diameter. Consequently, its intensity—or if you like, its concentration—becomes *four hundred trillion* times weaker than at the point where we had interposed the white surface.

Obviously, we are far from having realized an artificial sun in this way. The light that envelops the planet is of the weakest. No human eye could perceive this insignificant addition to the already weak illumination of the starry sky.

However, we must not think that this light, four hundred trillion times weaker than a ray of sunlight, is nothing. Just as optics provides methods for preventing the dispersion of rays at their departure, it can also concentrate those rays on their arrival.

The procedures are ancient, since we know that in binoculars and telescopes the rays scattered over the surface of the objective—either lens or mirror—concentrate themselves at the focal point, where they acquire an intensity proportional to the concentration, except for weakening by refraction or reflection.

We could perhaps assess directly the concentration and increase of intensity in these devices. But the calculations would be complicated and difficult, and would, besides, not really be conclusive. Fortunately, we can turn to a completely different order of proof.

It concerns the visibility of luminous phenomena from one planet to another. Now, the natural phenomena recorded by astronomy will permit us to assess directly, in numerical form, the possibility of exchanging signals.

§6. The planet Neptune turns around the Sun at a distance thirty times greater than that of Earth to the same star. This planet is easily visible in a telescope of medium strength. It has a satellite, which we have been able to observe, although it is naturally much smaller.

Supposing that Neptune reflects a *fifth* of the light it receives from the Sun, we can determine through a rather simple calculation that the light that reaches Earth is more than *two hundred trillion* times weaker than a ray of sunlight.

Taking the intensity of the Sun on Earth as a unity, we have then in numbers, for the illuminating intensity of Neptune:

$$\frac{1}{200,000,000,000,000}$$

And for that of the signal proposed above:

$$\frac{1}{400,000,000,000,000}$$

The comparison of these two fractions shows immediately that *the light of the signal is only two times weaker than that of Neptune seen from Earth.*

§7. This is an encouraging proportion, but the difficulty is not entirely overcome, even though we could still hope for a result, even under such conditions.

Is there a way of increasing this overly weak intensity? Without a doubt, and the method is quite easy to imagine.

All that is needed is to aim simultaneously two, three, four, or ten similar light beams at the same planet to make the light two, three, four, or ten times more intense. The rays will all relate to the same apparent point, if the lamps that send them are next to one another. However, this point will become brighter for the observers, the more lamps there are.

In this way, with two electric lamps, we shall create on some dark part on the Earth's disk an artificial star, which, seen from Venus or Mars, will be approximately of the eighth magnitude.

§8. A conical base only twenty million meters in diameter might demand a precision in the instruments beyond what could be achieved in practice. In that case, we will have to calculate according to a larger diameter and increase the number of lamps in proportion to the square of this diameter.

In admitting the number of two lamps for twenty million meters, it follows that for forty million meters, we would need eight lamps; for a hundred million, fifty lamps.

The maximum diameter needed to reach the targeted planet with certainty and the minimum diameter possible according to the instruments will be positively determined in the practical discussions of the project. I limit myself at present to the approximate information I have given above, simply to show that the difficulties are humanly surmountable. The calculations to be made for this purpose are, moreover, simple trigonometry problems, whose explicit solutions I shall give if asked.

Finally, I should note one indispensable condition for the functioning of the devices. Each mirror must be mounted on a parallactic gearwheel, which will compensate for the effects of the Earth's rotation, as well as for the effects of the sidereal revolutions of both planets.

§9. One question, which I will not consider thoroughly here in order to avoid overly technical details, is that of the places to be chosen on Earth, for the transmission and subsequent reception of the signals.

The areas near the poles seem to me to combine many advantages; among others, long nights that would permit uninterrupted connections for months at a time, even with the two inner planets. On the contrary, in the regions near the equator we would have only short periods of dawn and dusk to send signals to those planets. As for the outer planets, the only inconvenience of the equatorial regions would be their often cloudy skies and the need to interrupt the signals during the day.

However, I am not absolutely convinced that it would be impossible to make the signals bright enough to be seen on the illuminated surface of Earth, as *brighter* points than the neighboring areas. In that case, we could take as our luminous source the Sun itself, whose rays would be reflected and concentrated by mirrors.

II

§1. Let us imagine that mankind has realized the project. The inhabitants of Venus or Mars, if they have refracting or reflecting telescopes, or some other instruments for magnifying celestial bodies, can see, on the dark edge of the Earth's disk, a point of light. It is the signal that men are sending them.

If asked, observers might think that the point of light is either an active volcano or some other unexplained optical effect; in a word, a natural phenomenon demonstrating no will but the unfathomable universal will. After that, if the signal remained that way, as an immobile and constantly shining point, nothing would prevent it from being considered as a new astronomical fact, worthy of being noticed and recorded, but nothing more.

§2. It is important then that the signal not have this character, but that it undergo changes so that its *intentional* origin and its purpose not remain in doubt.

These changes will be simply special intermittent patterns that we shall now determine.

Appearances and disappearances following a simple periodic pattern would not disprove the idea of an astronomical phenomenon, most of which are intermittent and regularly rhythmic. Produced randomly, these variations would probably only serve to corroborate the explanation of a volcano erupting at different times.

Let me also add that we should avoid wasting time by transmitting signals for no other purpose than attracting attention. We can do better, and this is how.

§3. I must say first of all—and the rest of this study justifies my opinion—that the first notion to be exchanged is that of *numeration*.

Now, the first signals must have a character that is *alive* in some way, and that expresses the law of numeration that we shall use later.

A discussion of the system of numeration to be used, demanding absolutely special mathematical notions, can enter this memoir only if I attempt to make it accessible to all. It will suffice to say that the system must be as simple as possible at the beginning, even if it is to change later. The usual system, with nine significant figures plus zero, must be rejected because of its complications; the values of its elementary figures are too high—which also makes the sum of the figures of a given number too high—and the entirely conventional use of zero is difficult to guess.

We must use very few elementary signs and utilize all of their possible arrangements in the order of their generation.

The elementary figures will be: a single flash, a double flash, a triple flash, etc.

§4. If we limit ourselves to three elementary signs, this is the order of appearances there should be in the first signals; appearances are represented by dots, with spaces proportional to the lengths of disappearances:

.   ..   .
    ...   .   etc., etc.

The most basic study of this series reveals its rule. It is a sequence of different groups composed of one, two, and three elementary terms, and so on; and these elementary terms are of only three kinds: a single flash, a double flash, and a triple flash. Consecutive groups of these terms replace each other, following their order of magnitude. This system can be continued indefinitely and can be used to represent the series of natural numbers. The properties, incidentally quite interesting, of this extremely simple numeration, and of other similar numerations, must be the subject of a special study.

To eliminate any possible doubt, we shall need to produce, after a sequence of representative groups, a sequence of the numbers they represent—each of these numbers being expressed by as many single flashes as the unities it contains. Finally, we shall add a few examples, such as a rather large number expressed by successive flashes, followed by its representation in the adopted numerical system.

§5. The preceding example of the first signals to be given was made with a numeration using *three* elements. I did not mean to imply that this system is preferable. Perhaps a numeration with *two* elements is more advantageous. It remains a question that will require rigorous examination. The conclusion of this study will probably tend toward the use of a numeration based on a few elementary signs. I shall note that here we have questions of maximum and minimum values whose solutions become unimportant, since they would be the same, if the beings corresponding with us are at our approximate intellectual level.

§6. These then will be the first signals to send. We shall need to repeat them constantly, varying the examples of numerical representation; for doing so too rarely would lessen our chances of being seen by those we are signaling. If the call had been made to Earth, it too would have required frequent repetitions, since our scientists have not been taking turns at their instruments unceasingly to observe the surfaces of other planets.

Perhaps we shall wait a long time for a reply; perhaps too we shall tire of the attempt before the reply arrived. Nevertheless, we would have no right to conclude that the plan is irrational, nor that the planets are uninhabited except by beings inferior to man.

Imagine a call made to Earth, under the conditions I have given, before Galileo; it would have been absolutely impossible for anyone to have noticed or answered.

This consideration suffices to establish that a first unsuccessful attempt must not be seen as a reason to stop. The signals might have been seen, and even understood, but no reply made due to a lack of material means.

If the call were made to Earth today, before we could answer it, we would have to overcome the ignorance, skepticism, and ill will of many men, and then proceed with the delicate, difficult, and expensive construction of the apparatuses for transmission. There would be much time lost, and the senders would probably give up on us out there.

§7. But let us put aside these negative predictions and continue our discussion.

Observers, armed with the most powerful instruments, keep their eyes on the interrogated planet. Then, on the dark portion of its disk, a small point of light appears. It is the response! This point of light, by its intermittent patterns based on the Earth's signal, seems to say, "We have seen you; we have understood you."

It will be a moment of joy and pride for mankind. The eternal isolation of the spheres is vanquished. No more limit to our avid human curiosity, which, already impatient, was pacing the Earth, like a tiger in its narrow cage.

But in this intoxication, as we dream of hastening the day when we shall know all, a reflection arises and frightens us. These dreams are based on a tiny light shining far away, in a world where everything, no doubt, is different than it is down here. The light tells us that someone is out there, but nothing more. We want to know everything, we want to see, hear, and touch this mysterious world. The little light only aggravates our thirst for knowledge and makes it intolerable. Can a world appear to us in this almost imperceptible light?

That is what remains to be seen.

§8. Yes, this little light is enough to transport one world into another. The patterns of its appearances and disappearances can embody all conceivable perceptible essences. And there is nothing miraculous or strange about that.

Once the method of numeration is adopted by both sides, mankind can, if we like, begin explicit communication.

We only know how to transmit numbers; therefore, we shall use numbers to understand each other. Now, this limit being established, there is only one method to follow. We must translate, by a simple geometric procedure, appropriately selected plane figures into numerical series, and transmit successively the terms of these series.

Mathematicians know many graphic procedures, by which a plane figure—or even a solid—can be represented in segments by a series of numbers; reciprocally, they know how to translate a series of numbers into a figure constructed of points. These different graphic methods must then be graded, so that we can choose the simplest of them.

If the question remains unresolved between four or five of these procedures, there would be minimal inconvenience. Those receiving the signal would only need to try them all; they would finally find the one used by the senders.

In order to make myself understood by all, I shall show by a familiar example how a numerical series can represent a plane figure, or any drawing.

The series of numbers:

$$19 \quad 3 \quad 7 \quad 1 \quad 1 \quad 4 \quad 25$$

being given in writing, we take a thread of indefinite length and pearls of two colors—black and white, if we like. We read the first number, 19, and thread nineteen pearls of the same color on the thread—white pearls, for example; we read the second number, 3, and thread three black pearls. And so on for the other numbers, alternating the colors of the pearls. In this way we have a string of pearls, in which black and white follow each other, with no apparent meaning to their succession.

We fill another thread according to the second series:

18   4   6   2   5   6   19.

We do the same for a third and fourth series, and so on until the last one.

That done, it will not take much effort to imagine putting the strings of pearls next to one another, in the same order as the series had been given. In this way, we shall see on the surface covered with pearls a fairly detailed figure formed by black pearls, with the white pearls serving as a background. This is the drawing made with points that the series implicitly contained.

Procedures similar to this numerical notation of drawings are used in various industries, such as weaving and embroidery. It is a whole science, which, following the usual course, was practiced before being systematized. A new and important branch of mathematics will come from it, and after that a new classification of those essential sciences. The study of *rhythms* will take its place at the same level as that of *figures*.

If we stopped with the method I have just described, transmission would be very simple. We would send, by means of our previously established numeration, first one series of numbers; then, after a sufficiently long pause, another series, and so on.

This method of transmission is not the only one; nor do I think it the best, and I chose it merely as an example that is easy to describe. We could also thread the pearls, one after another, and wrap the thread around a cylinder, knowing the number of pearls to thread for each turn, or turn the thread in a spiral on a flat surface, having determined the rule for increasing the number of pearls in each turn.

I repeat, there are a great many graphic methods, all of which need to be discussed in detail. I have done some work in this direction, and shall publish it later, if necessary.

There is, at any rate, no immediate difficulty, and we have more than enough time to fix the details.

§9. The transmission of periodic flashes is thus brought in this way to the transmission of drawings, of planar projections. It remains for us then to examine briefly whether this method of communication will satisfy all the requirements of the work that I propose.

I have been told that transmission in this way is very slow; we must however be satisfied with it if there is no other. Let me say, however, that in addition to the conventions of abbreviation we shall establish later, I predict that extremely rapid methods of transmission could be implemented.

In fact, if we color the rays differently, each element of the numeration will become a single flash whose color alone will indicate its value. Or else a given signal will have a different value for each of its possible colors.

To that, we must add the possibility of polarizing the light according to all the angles of the dial, or of passing it through fumes whose spectral analysis will reveal its nature at the place of its arrival.

These resources seem to promise an interplanetary language as rapid and precise as its supreme importance will require.

III

§1. I have very little to add to what I have already said on the subject.

Two worlds exchange signs equivalent to drawn figures; the result is easily predictable, and guidance is not very useful. Every scientist, every man on Earth, will give his opinion, and perhaps those will produce some idea far better than any I could suggest at the moment.

I shall limit myself then to a few prehistoric outlines on the subject.

§2. It will be necessary to construct a sequence of figures representing the totality of human knowledge. Each of these figures will be designated by a number—as far as possible in a scientific order going from simple notions to notions that are more and more complex. Besides, this order will result from the necessity of being understood. Thus, the expression of one element of human knowledge, once its representative figure is transmitted, will be the number that designates this figure.

§3. An example will clarify this.

We want to distinguish and name colors; we make a clear and simple drawing showing the experiment of separating colors with a prism. The mixed ray in this figure gives rise to many single rays. We number, on the same figure, the different rays in the order of their ascending refrangibility. The total figure is itself designated by a number; let us suppose that it is plate 17. Group 17-1 will mean red, 17-2 orange, 17-6 blue, etc.

Thus the number 17 will signify *color* in general, and the following number will indicate the specific color.

In the same way we shall transmit and name the notions of chemical substances, different physical forces, musical elements, vocal sounds, etc., by their numerical differential aspects.

It is useless, for the moment, to continue this presentation; it would be inappropriate to go into further detail. The figurative representation of human knowledge forms a special, and extremely vast, study that would lead us too far afield. Besides, it deserves to be treated separately, and will require many collaborators for its elaboration.

Moreover, this ideographic work will have had precedents, although previous work pursued a different goal than our current one.

§4. I sense an objection raised since the beginning of this presentation; I should respond before I close.

Am I the only one, in the crowd of neighboring worlds, to have imagined the sequence of ideas expressed here? Probably not. So, if these ideas are not idle reveries, why has no signal been addressed to Earth, why have warnings not come to us from beings who undoubtedly possess more powerful means than ours; for there must be such beings in the infinity of possibilities?

We saw earlier that for a long time human society remained incapable of perceiving signals and understanding them. Perhaps signals have been sent, and mankind has not seen them; perhaps they are being sent to us today, and we pay no attention. Physical astronomy is still studied with so little enthusiasm that such phenomena could pass unnoticed,

Chance has placed a few strange facts before my eyes; I wanted to see them assembled, I wanted them to be searched for, to see if they would appear again.

Various observers, Schröter, Harding, Messier, and others, have seen points of light on the disks of Mercury, Mars, and even, as I recall, on Venus.

Explanations that suppose volcanoes, or ill-defined phenomena of reflected solar rays, are not satisfactory, as everyone concedes.

Let us watch attentively; perhaps we shall see these points again and see them better. We need a preconceived idea in order to see them, and we have not had that until now.

§5. I have finished saying what I think is most immediately important about the question I have raised, and I am ready to explain all the details, as far as I can, if the question is discussed seriously.

I shall be happy if I am not confronted on every side, as has often happened before, by an ignorant denial of everything that is not a faithful copy of the past.

SUPPORTING NOTE

Evaluation of the intensity of Neptune's light seen from Earth.—Take, as a unit l, the quantity of light received from the Sun, on Earth, by a surface of one square meter at a normal to the rays.

Let us determine the number of these luminous units emitted by the Sun and intercepted by Neptune.

Neptune's ray is:

28,380,000 meters.

We derive from it the surface of a great circle:

$(28,380,000)2 \times \pi = 2,530,321,295,040,000$ square meters.

The quantity of light received being, on an equal surface, 902 times less on Neptune than on Earth, we find for the number of intercepted luminous units:

2,811,000,000,000 *l*.

We admit that metallic mirrors reflect approximately *one third* of the light they receive; we can therefore fix confidently at *one fifth* the quantity of light reflected by the much less absorbent surface of a planet. Therefore we have, for the number of reflected units,

562,500,000,000 *l*.

This quantity of light expands in space, distributing itself equally onto the inner surface of an ideal hemisphere having Neptune as its center. The more the radius of this hemisphere—that is to say, the distance to Neptune—increases, the more the light disperses and weakens. Let us measure this dispersal.

In round numbers, the distance from Neptune to Earth is

4,500,000,000,000 meters.

Taking the square of this number and multiplying it by 2π, we obtain the hemispheric surface for which this distance is the radius. We find for this surface:

127,234,395,000,000,000,000,000,000 square meters.

The light emitted by Neptune will undergo, arriving on Earth, a weakening proportional to this number. We have seen that Neptune emits

$$562,500,000,000$$

units of light; the illuminating intensity of this planet on Earth—or the quantity of light that a meter on the surface receives—will therefore be expressed by the following fraction:

$$\frac{5,625\,l}{1,272,343,950,000,000,000}$$

which becomes, once reduced:

$$\frac{l}{226,194,480,000,000.}$$

This is the *minimum* value—in the case of transmitted signals—of the intensity of the source divided by the portion of the beam that reaches the planet's surface.

METHODS OF MUSICAL STENOGRAPHY AND NEW DEVICES INTENDED FOR THE EXACT GRAPHIC NOTATION OF MUSIC PLAYED ON KEYBOARD INSTRUMENTS, BY MESSIEURS CHARLES ÉMILE HORTENSIUS CROS AND ANTOINE HIPPOLYTE CROS IN PARIS

. . . .

The principal object of our invention is the realization of the following idea: to notate by stenographic transcription, as accurately as desired, music played on a keyboard instrument. This accuracy is due primarily to the uniformity of the continuous motions used; a uniformity no longer broken by variations in friction. We obtain this result by several new methods, to which we also claim exclusive rights as essential elements of our invention. These various methods can be divided into two types:

First type of device—Musical stenographer—System of mechanical transmission.

This device is essentially composed of four parts, whose descriptions follow:

1. A system of levers, as many as the notes on a keyboard instrument. The levers, made of some rigid material, are

placed horizontally, with their fulcrums near their centers, on a crossbar. They are of different lengths; they affect a converging disposition in the models applicable to pianos or parlor organs, and become, following the geometric law, longer as they become more oblique. Each ends in a sharp point, where resistance occurs in ways we shall describe later; the power acts on the larger end in such a way that it lowers the point each time. We call these instruments *transmission levers*.

These levers need to move silently; which is easy to obtain with padding of flannel, rubber, cork, cloth, etc., applied wherever any noisy impact might occur. Their positions also must change as little as possible; which we have obtained, in the realization of our idea, by passing both the points and larger ends through small openings cut in fixed wooden bollards. It is, moreover, indispensable that their fulcrums be immovable, and yet that they be able to move freely on these fulcrums, but always in the same vertical plane. A small iron pivot passing through a somewhat longer opening, placed approximately in the middle of each lever, is the method we chose to fulfill this condition.

2. Rigid vertical rods, free on both ends, but padded on both ends with material able to withstand impact without making noise, held in place by a suitably disposed wooden chassis, establish the connection between the

keyboard instrument and our device. The lower end of each rod transmits to the lever that rests on its higher end the action of the key corresponding to the note that is to be notated graphically. The adaptation is extremely easy for both pianos and organs. We call these elements *transmission rods*.

3. The pointed ends of the levers are meant to activate the actual graphic device.

To obtain the goal that we set for ourselves, that is, to represent *rigorously* the value and duration of the notes that are played, we can employ three graphic systems that will not cause variation in the friction, and consequently, in the speed imparted to a strip of paper by the ensemble of rollers described further below. The first system consists of a series of little levers or graphic appendages armed at each end with two blunt points, one *marking*, the other *non-marking*. Springs keep the non-marking points lowered to the paper; in this way the paper is subjected to a given friction. When one or several keys of the keyboard instrument are activated, the movement produced is transmitted by the vertical rods to the converging horizontal levers; the latter then press the graphic appendages on the ends with the marking points; these points lower and make the desired marks on the paper. But when a marking point is lowered, the corresponding non-marking point is raised, reducing the total resistance by as much as the marking point had increased it. One can see that this mechanical arrangement permits an invariable degree of friction.

The second system consists of a series of tubes ending in cannulas or ruling pens; each of these tubes communicates with a small compressible reservoir containing some kind of ink. The little reservoirs can be hollow solids of some elastic material like vulcanized rubber, or cylinders equipped with spring-loaded pistons. It is understood that since all these ruling pens or cannulas are applied constantly to the paper, no mark will be made if the reservoirs are not pressed, and the ink will not reach the end in contact with the paper.

When the pens are activated, however, the marks will be made without any variation in friction. The converging levers will serve to apply precisely the necessary pressure on the reservoirs whenever activated. Suitable stops will be required to limit the pressure of the levers, in order to control the propulsion of the ink.

The third system consists of a series of holes or windows cut into an opaque partition, and closed by means of spring-loaded covers. The converging levers open these windows whenever they are activated by the playing of the keys. A lamp, with or without reflector, is placed before the opaque partition where the windows are cut; behind this partition, in the path of the light rays, is another strip of paper—or any other surface—*sensitive to light* and moved by clockwork. Slits arranged appropriately in the opaque partition inscribe continually on the photographic surface the readings that were obtained in the preceding systems by an inked roller. When the levers move, the corresponding windows open, allowing the passage of light beams, which will expose the photographic surface without interrupting or delaying its movement in any way. With this system, reduction is possible and unlimited because, if necessary, it can even be rendered microscopic by means of a converging lens. The photographic surface must be sensitized so that it produces marks instantaneously by the known methods.

4. Finally, the fourth inherent part of the device places under the action of the graphic system, with a uniform and consistent motion, a strip of lined paper that will be described further below, on which the marks corresponding to the sounds are to be collected and fixed.

It consists of a clockwork movement that opposes, in the manner of a rolling mill, two cylinders whose movement pulls the strip of paper. This strip unwinds from a mobile axis on which it has been previously wound. It passes over two little rollers acting as pulleys, which keep it on the horizontal plane and at the desired distances from the different elements we have just described. The strip passes intact over the first roller-pulley, arrives at the graphic device, receives the colored imprints notating the sounds that are played, and then passes, marked in this way, over the second roller-pulley; it is then fed into the space between the cylinders, and leaves the device by an opening cut into the box that houses it.

Second type of device—Musical stenographer—System based solely on the chemical action of galvanic currents.

When a metal wire is placed in contact with paper that is suitably prepared and attached to a conductive surface, and if the wire is attached to one pole of a battery while the conductive surface is attached to the other pole, a colored mark is produced on the paper that is interposed in the current. If the communication is broken, a mark will no longer be made, even if the wire remains in contact with the paper. It is understood that by attaching each key on the piano to a metal wire equipped with a switch arranged so that the current flows only when the corresponding key is depressed, one will obtain, greatly reduced if needed, the precise graphic notation of every action imprinted on the keys of the instrument. The conditions relating to the other parts of the graphic device remain the same as in the first type.

The endless paper intended to receive the marks carries two systems of lines: one in the direction of the paper's length, the other in the direction of its width. The first serves to identify readily the pitch of the inscribed note, the second is intended to mark its relative duration. A printing roller, constantly impregnated with a suitable ink, allows the paper to be lined immediately before or after the impression made by the graphic system in the device itself. The lines running lengthwise are of three kinds: lines of asterisks serving to indicate the beginning and end of octaves; the interval between two lines represents a *whole step*; the interval between a line and a space represents a *half step*. In this way, each of the twelve pitches of the scale on keyboard instruments has a distinct place in a system of three solid lines and three dotted lines. The lines running widthwise are all similar and equidistant; they serve to mark and measure the durations of notes and rests.

In summary, we claim, whether as new applications of old laws, or as improved realizations of formerly conceived ideas:

1. The idea of obtaining the *precise* notation—as far as possible—of music while it is being played, an idea conceived by us alone and realized by us alone, no doubt to varying degrees, but by methods that are all quite sufficient in practice, and most of them close to absolute mathematical perfection;

2. We claim the different types of devices, either described in the present paper or illustrated in the diagrams that we attach, as well as all new inherent details, indicated as such in this work, and all eventual modifications permitting variations in construction and changes in form and dimension, according to secondary

considerations of convenience, arrangement, easy transport, and even elegance, but especially concerning adaptation to different kinds of keyboard instruments;

3. We claim the application, to the ends that we set for ourselves, of physical laws not yet exploited for this purpose, namely: Pascal's principle, the chemical properties of light, and the chemical properties of galvanic currents employed without transmission of any actual motions;

4. Finally, we claim the application of our methods to the *direct* or *indirect* reproduction of music written with the help of our instruments, on cylinders of so-called barrel organs, or other instruments of the same type, a reproduction that could be obtained easily without errors, without guesswork, without translation, and without calculation.

TRANSLATOR'S NOTES

"La Science de l'amour" first appeared in *La Revue du monde nouveau* (April 1874), was reprinted in *Le Chat noir* (17 October, 24 October, 31 October, and 7 November 1885), and then in *Le Collier de griffes*.

Étienne-Jules Marey was a physiologist and, like Cros, a member of the Académie des Sciences and a pioneer in photography. In 1882, he was to invent the chronophotographic gun, a forerunner of the movie camera.

Louis Henri Rosellen's "Trois Rêveries" were published in 1841. The first, nicknamed "Le Trémolo," became a salon chestnut.

The ditty about the fetus enjoying his alcohol presages Maurice Mac-Nab's "Les fœtus," one of his most celebrated songs at the Chat Noir.

Johannes Secundus's *Liber Basiorum* (1514) is a collection of poems about kisses.

Joris-Karl Huysmans cites "La Science de l'Amour" in his novel *À rebours*, where he praises its humor, but censures its unpoetic style—a curious objection, given the narrator's decidedly prosaic personality.

"Un drame interastral" was published in *La Renaissance littéraire et artistique* (24 August 1874), and then in *Le Chat noir* (7 August 1886).

Curiously, it was not included in either of Cros's collections. It has long been a favorite of Cros's admirers; the Collège de Pataphysique declared it a "texte canonique."

"Le Journal de l'avenir" first appeared in *Le Chat noir* (13 March 1886) but was based on a story Cros had previously published in *Tout-Paris* (23 May 1880). It was reprinted in *Le Collier de griffes*.

Jules Grévy was then president of France, and presumably too busy to frequent the Chat Noir. Rodolphe Salis was the founder, proprietor, and host of the cabaret, and Alphonse Allais was the editor of its weekly paper.

Sarah Bernhardt was a favorite among Parisian Bohemians and admitted as an honorary Hydropathe.

The American inventors Tadblagson and Humbugson are swipes at Edison, whom Cros never forgave for beating him to the patent office.

The poet Théodore de Banville was known for his experiments with poetic form. His collaborator here is Jacques Cujas, a legal scholar of the sixteenth century.

"Le Caillou mort d'amour" was published in *Le Chat noir* (20 March 1886), in the collection *Les Gaités du Chat noir* (Ollendorff, 1894), and then in *Le Collier de griffes*.

Plato describes the music of the spheres in *The Republic*, Book 10, Section 14.

"Diamant enfumé" first appeared in *Le Chat noir* (20 December 1884) and was reprinted in *Le Collier de griffes*. The woman described is Nina de Villard, with whom Cros had a long and complicated liaison. Cros also wrote a poem with the same title, about the same Nina, which he included in *Le Coffret de santal*.

"La Chanson de la plus belle femme" first appeared in *Le Chat noir* (7 February 1885), and then in *Le Collier de griffes*. Judging from its style, it was probably written several years before publication.

"Les Gens de lettres" was published in *Le Chat noir* (10 July 1886), and then in *Le Collier de griffes*. The mention of the "salt herring" recalls Cros's monologue of the same name, also intended for children.

"Distrayeuse" and the following five pieces were published in *Le Coffret de santal* as "Fantaisies en prose." "Distrayeuse" first appeared in *La Renaissance littéraire et artistique* (21 September 1872), and later in *Le Chat noir* (28 August, 1886). The word "distrayeur" is rare, and Cros seems to have been the first to use the feminine form.

"Le Meuble" was published in *La Renaissance littéraire et artistique* (18 May 1872), and then in *Le Chat noir* (11 September 1886). The cabinet belonged to the grandmother of Mathilde Mauté, the wife of Paul Verlaine. She described it in her *Mémoires*: "It was an Henri II cabinet in carved solid ebony, the interior decorated with little mirrors and white and green ivory lozenges, which I still possess; it contains two secret drawers."

"Madrigal" was published in *La Renaissance littéraire et artistique* (27 July 1872). Dame Emma Hamilton (originally Amy Lyon) was a famous beauty of the late eighteenth century, celebrated in many paintings by George Romney. The fan was most likely Cros's invention.

"Sur Trois Aquatintes" was first published in *Le Coffret de santal*. Henry Cros might have created aquatints on these subjects, but none has survived. He did produce both watercolor and glass paste renditions of Venus drawn by seahorses, and a watercolor of the piano-boat, reported to be in the collection of Henri Matarasso. The name Igitur was probably taken from Mallarmé's story of the same name, at that point unpublished but read and discussed in Cros's circle.

"L'Heure froide" first appeared in *Le Coffret de santal* and was re-printed in *Le Chat noir* (9 October 1886). Count Ferdinand de Strada was a friend of the Cros family; he was no doubt related to Édouard de Strada, who collaborated with Antoine Cros on the book *Demain, pensées politiques pour la rénovation de France: écrites pendant le Siège de Paris* (1872).

"Lassitude" was first published in *Le Coffret de santal*.

Cros read his "Étude sur les moyens de communication avec les planètes" to the Académie des Sciences on 5 July 1869. It was se-rialized in the scientific journal *Cosmos* in August, and then printed as a booklet.

Johann Schröter (1745–1816) directed an observatory at Lilienthal; he made many drawings of Mars and the Moon. Karl Ludwig Harding (1765–1834) directed an observatory at Göttingen and discovered the asteroid Juno. Charles Messier (1730–1817) published a catalogue of nebulae and star clusters, and discovered so many comets that Louis XV nicknamed him the "Ferret of Comets."

Alphonse Allais, in his story "Ohé! Ohé!" (*Le Journal*, 13 November 1894), proposed that Cros's light signals be supplemented with loud noises, to get the aliens' attention.

"Procédés de stenographie musicale et appareils nouveaux destinés à la représentation graphique exacte de la musique exécutée sur les instruments à clavier, par Messieurs Charles Émile Hortensius Cros et Antoine Hippolyte Cros à Paris" was patented 10 May 1864 (Patent no. 62974). Two copies in Antoine's hand have survived, marked as intended for a planned collection of Charles's scientific writings. The text was first published in Pierre E. Richard's edition of Cros's *Inédits et Documents* (1992), unfortunately without the explanatory drawings. The Cros brothers apparently made no attempt to market it.

They were neither the first nor the last to imagine a notating keyboard. Marie Bobillier (as Michel Brenet) cites several in her *Dictionnaire pratique et historique de la musique* (1926), including Creed (1747), Hohlfeld and Muger (1750), Pape (1824), Eisenmenger (1836), Guérin (1843), Rivoire (1895), and Barbieri (1909).

Doug Skinner has contributed to *Fortean Times*, *Cabinet*, *Nickelodeon*, *Weirdo*, *Fate*, *Black Scat Review*, *Strange Attractor Journal*, and other magazines. Among his books are *The Snowman Three Doors Down*, *Sleepytime Cemetery*, *Nominata*, and translations of Alphonse Allais, Charles Cros, Alfred Jarry, Pierre-Corneille Blessebois, Giovanni Battista Nazari, and Luigi Russolo.

IMAGING SCIENCE